AI,

"Relationships matter more than ever. *AI and the New Oz* provides an excellent roadmap for the people-first approach required to navigate the inevitable challenges of AI adoption and to maximize its potential. The book is a clever and engaging adaptation of the Wizard of Oz narrative for leaders who understand that the core qualities of leadership – courage, wisdom, heart, and vision – are crucial qualities for every leader in the age of AI."

Carole Robin, PhD, Co-Author of the award-winning *Connect*; former Director, Arbuckle Leadership Fellows program, Stanford Graduate School of Business; Co-Founder, Leaders in Tech

"In the current chaotic birth of AI for Everyone, Tonya provides sage wisdom and advice for leaders and consumers of this new technology. The democratization of AI to the masses will be the pivot point of no return. Using Characterization and the story of the Wizard of Oz, we are guided through a journey, much like Dorothy, that will teach us how to embrace the changing landscape, which includes GenAI as well as other ML/AI innovations. With this new-found understanding, we can step boldly into the new tech landscape shaped by AI with confidence and some roadside directions."

Morgan Templar, Chief Executive Officer, First CDO Partners and Author, *Get Governed* and *A Culture of Governance*

"The people-first approach to AI adoption that Tonya J. Long outlines in her book AI and the New Oz resonates with me deeply because she integrates ethics and empowerment into her vision for an AI-enabled future. This book is an invaluable resource for leaders because it not only offers empathy and encouragement, it outlines tangible steps every leader can take to lead their teams to that future with brains, heart, and courage."

Elisa Camahort Page, Co-Founder of BlogHer and Author, *Road Map for Revolutionaries: Resistance, Activism, and Advocacy for All*

"Artificial Intelligence isn't a futuristic concept for 'some day'; it's our reality, revolutionizing how we do business right now. Recent Gartner data shows a stark contrast between organizations initiating AI projects and those actually deploying them (79% vs 21%). AI and the New Oz is more than a book – it's a blueprint for leaders to mobilize their teams and engage fully with AI integration. This isn't solely about supercharging our businesses; it's about embracing our roles as architects of a broader, AI-influenced society."

Steven Griset, Chief Technology Officer and Co-Founder, AlwaysAI

AI AND THE NEW OZ

"Disruptive technologies like GenAI have accelerated humanity with a level of expertise that matches, if not exceeds, human capabilities. Adapting to this change is one of our greatest challenges. AI and the New Oz is a playful and engaging way of using archetypes to address the traits we must embrace to remain relevant. When history is written, we'll find that our collective humanity elevated AI to achieve great things for our world. Leadership is key to transformation, and this book's common-sense approach is a playbook for enabling people, process, culture and industry as we evolve."

Marko Jak, Co-Founder, Secta AI Labs

"AI and the New Oz is an engaging view of how leaders will deliver AI into the future, but I valued something else others will appreciate. I thoroughly enjoyed the book because it makes the AI conversation truly accessible to those of us who aren't "techies," and that's an important part of moving everyone forward.

Tonya has definitely been part of the "ground team" so reading the book was like experiencing a first-hand account of the major moments that delivered us to this point. Her enthusiasm and storytelling make this a fun read, and I feel more connected to what this all means. People who aren't on the front lines will benefit from the context - and they'll lead differently."

Dr. Heather Backstrom, Founder of Backstrom Leadership Strategies
and Bestselling Author, *Collaborative Confidence*

"As someone who finds joy in intellectual playfulness, AI *and the New Oz* offers a playground for the mind. The book challenges readers to engage with the complex tapestry of artificial intelligence and its considerations for adoption in the future of work. Tonya's clarion call to leadership truly comes from the heart as she beckons others to step up to the challenge to bring society forward with sweeping changes to how we live, work, and play."

Bruce Taub, Founder, Publisher and CEO, *The Principal Post*

Al and the New Oz

AI and the New Oz

Leadership's Journey to the Future of Work

TONYA J. LONG
with GPT-4

Copyright © 2023 by Tonya J. Long.

All rights reserved. No part of this book may be reproduced or used in any manner without the prior written permission of the copyright owner, except for the use of brief quotations embodied in critical articles or reviews.

Library of Congress Cataloging-in-Publication Data
Long, Tonya J., 1970 – author.
AI and the new oz: leadership's journey to the
future of work / Tonya J. Long with GPT-4

First Edition | San Jose, CA (2023)

Library of Congress Control Number: 2023912720
ISBN: 979-8-39809-844-0 *hardcover*
ISBN: 979-8-39781-347-1 *paperback*

Printed in the United States of America
Cover design by Tonya J. Long / iStock

Dedication

This book, my first, is dedicated to my parents. Their commitment, sense of community, unfailing work ethic, and love of people are the cornerstones of my life. Guided by my dad's analytical mind and fueled by my mom's limitless compassion, elevating others is my North Star.

The focus of my life's work and the essence of this book can be traced to their thoughtful influence more than fifty years ago. They instilled in me a profound appreciation for the diverse contributions of individuals and cultivated an unwavering commitment to advocate for the rights of others to make meaningful contributions to society. I wrote this book to encourage leaders to embrace the power of diverse perspectives and champion the meaningful impact of *every* individual.

Mom & Dad, circa 1967

AI and collective intelligence represents an incredible opportunity to enable a future that fosters connection, innovation, and a sense of purpose. May this journey inspire us to build the brighter, more inclusive future we've all been dreaming of.

Contents:
AI and the New Oz

Foreword	XI
Introduction	1
1. The Yellow Brick Road to AI Adoption	15
2. Dorothy's Eye for Talent	39
3. The Cowardly Lion's Bravery	51
4. The Tin Man's Heart to #LeadwithLove	65
5. The Scarecrow's Quest for Wisdom	79
6. The Wizard's Vision	99
7. The Wicked Witch of Resistance	109
8. The Munchkin Land of Collaboration	127
9. There's No Place Like Home	143
Acknowledgments	151
Notes	153
About the Author	163

~~FOREWORD~~ Prologue

ONCE UPON A TIME, these three pages held the words of an insightful Foreword written by a valued colleague and a true believer of a future that thoughtfully blends technology and humanity. Alas, a travel alert on the Yellow Brick Road has triggered a detour.

Now our journey begins here, at a historical watershed moment, where the dialogue about Artificial Intelligence has rapidly escalated to global action. From whispers in tech corridors to loud proclamations on striking picket lines, the discourse surrounding AI has taken center stage and turned predictions into reality faster than anticipated.

If you think AI doesn't matter in your field, at your level, or in your corner of the world, it's time to think again. This conversation has never been more relevant or more important.

Artificial Intelligence is no longer a distant concept, restricted to advanced technology labs or science fiction chatter. It's woven into the fabric of our societies, economies, and personal lives. The conversation about AI's impact, potential, and ethics – previously reserved for technologists and futurists – is now a responsibility we all share.

The chapters ahead hold more urgency today than when I first wrote them. The pace of AI integration into our lives is accelerating, outpacing even my initial predictions. With this rapid advance, it's natural to experience fear: fear of job loss, of decelerated careers, of a seismic shift in the way we conduct business. We know that when fear is unchecked or without context, it can lead to hasty reactions or unintended consequences. Knowing this, we must guard ourselves against it.

If you believe AI doesn't influence your world or you can't shape AI's role in your life, then it's time to rethink. More than ever, knowledge is our greatest ally. The wisdom to understand AI, to contribute meaningfully to its evolution, and to ensure its alignment with our values and goals is one of humanity's greatest opportunities. There is power in the knowledge of AI that enables us to navigate this new landscape, to ensure AI aligns with our values, our goals, and our shared humanity. AI *and the New* Oz will equip you with that power.

Our journey into the world of AI isn't about technology alone, **it's about empowerment.** It's about fostering a culture where individuals flourish, and teams feel supported in exploring their fullest potential. It's about leading with courage, heart, wisdom, and vision, as we redefine our business models and the future of work in an age of AI.

We stand on the edge of a new era. A New Oz awaits us, shaped by the promise of AI. This book is an invitation to you, to all of us, to actively participate in this journey. It's time to learn, to teach, to engage, and most importantly, to influence. Our responsibility is to ensure the narrative of AI is written by us, for us. This duty isn't mine or yours alone – **it's *our journey*,** #together.

This is a defining moment in our shared history. AI is real, it's here, and it's ours to shape. To each of you – *onward and upward.*

Our New Oz awaits.

Tonya J. Long
July 21, 2023

#LeadwithLove
#OnwardAndUpward

INTRODUCTION

"Toto, I've got a feeling we're not in Kansas anymore." - Dorothy

Remember the first time you saw *The Wizard of Oz*? You were probably pretty young and watched the movie on a family television. The adults at home may have been more excited about it than you were. In those days, the TV was the centerpiece in everyone's living rooms. For many of us, our first time watching L. Frank Baum's classic tale was a special event that we would repeat with our own families decades later.

Dorothy and Toto's whirlwind adventure is certainly timeless, and still a source of inspiration for many. In fact, the streaming series *Ted Lasso* just wrapped its third season in May of 2023 with countless nods to *The Wizard of Oz* story – unhappy with life in Kansas, running far away to look for something more, building a winning team from an unlikely group, and eventually realizing "there's no place like home."

Who doesn't love a story about facing the unknown, finding purpose, making a difference despite the obstacles, and returning to your roots happier than when you started? Most people remember the iconic songs and triumphant finale. But Dorothy's magical journey wasn't all fields of orange poppies and dancing to jingles. Do you remember how the movie began?

- **It was ominous.** Dark clouds were everywhere. A bad storm was coming and danger was on the horizon.

- **Everything was disconnected.** Dorothy couldn't find Toto; Aunt Em and Uncle Henry were in the cellar, but they couldn't reach Dorothy. Everyone was worried.

- **The unknown was frightening.** The sky turned green and the cyclone raced over the horizon toward Dorothy and Toto.

- **Then complete chaos broke loose.** The house flew into the air across the farmstead and windows shattered… while Dorothy clung to what mattered most, her beloved Toto.

And when the chaos and the darkness passed, after the stillness that followed… Dorothy's life changed.

Forever.

So did the lives of everyone she touched on her travels along the Yellow Brick Road, in the Emerald City, and on the journey to find her way home to Kansas.

Generative AI is progressing at an exponential pace

OpenAI estimates that the algorithmic capacity of generative AI is advancing in accordance with Moore's Law, but with a half-life of 3.4 months. This means that from 2012 to 2018, when the study was published, the algorithmic capacity has increased 300,000 times — and it's doubling every three and a half months.[1]

It's hard to wrap your head around numbers like that, but the bottom line is that the computing capacity of generative AI is growing exponentially. I wanted to understand how I could put that in context, so I asked GPT-4 to construct a table that started with a value of 100,000 and doubled every 3.4 months (~105 days) for a year.

Certainly! Here's the table as requested:

The table below shows the growth of a value starting at 100,000 and doubling every 105 days:

Date	Value	Increase	# Days (3.4 month cycle)	% Increase
Jan 1	100,000	-	-	-
Apr 16	200,000	100,000	105	100%
Jul 30	400,000	200,000	105	100%
Nov 12	800,000	400,000	105	100%
Dec 31	1,173,600	373,600	49	46.7%

As you can see, the value starts at 100,000 and doubles every 105 days. After a year, the value has increased to 1,173,600, which is an increase of 1,073,600 more than the original value of 100,000.

The results were even larger than I would have guessed. Interpreting GPT-4's explanation, if the capacity of our AI computing power was 100,000 in January, then – at the current rate of growth – the computing power would be 1,173,600 after 12 months. That's a **1,073% increase** in the algorithmic capacity in just a year.

You don't need programming skills to appreciate that rate of increase – or to consider what it would take to harness the power of that capability. The enormity starts to sink-in once you recognize the exponential growth because the numbers are significantly larger with every cycle. For example – if you run the same exercise for 2 years instead of just 12 months, the increase is 12,045%. These are enormous gains in AI capacity and they continue to grow.

Does this give you perspective about how much the capacity for growth is building, and how fast? If you're technically inclined and curious how it works, check out the OpenAI paper referenced in the first paragraph. The technical explanation is surprisingly straightforward for those who are around these conversations: better and more custom hardware that enables more computations to be performed, using newer higher-capacity chips (GPUs), running these chips in parallel to get increases by a factor of roughly 10x each year. Read the article; it's interesting and very consumable (and three years old at this point, so also consider how much faster things are moving today).

So, back to our story... Considering how all this began (in Kansas)... this leads to a few questions about what's happening today (with AI).

INTRODUCTION

- **Does it seem ominous?** Of course it does.

- **Are we disconnected and worried?** Seems like it. Raise your hand if you know (or are) someone who has lost sleep over what could happen with the rise of AI.

- **Does anyone think this is scary?** Sam Altman, OpenAI's CEO, said he was "a little bit scared" in a national television interview after the March release of GPT-4[2]. More recently, Sam Altman, Bill Gates, and a host of other technical luminaries signed a declaration[3] warning that "Mitigating the risk of extinction from AI should be a global priority alongside other societal-scale risks such as pandemics and nuclear war." Extinction?! Sounds pretty darn scary *and* ominous to me.

No one has experienced a technological change this large before. Other large-scale developments, like the introduction of the steam engine, electricity, and the automobile, occurred more than a century ago and evolved much more slowly. AI is transforming the world at breakneck speed, and we don't really have a game plan for this. Yet.

The generative AI journey is our next big adventure to the New Oz. I don't think the "AI cyclone" has crossed over the hill yet, so we still have time to gather Toto and the others and get back to the house. Just remember that the beginning was pretty bumpy: Dorothy had to get tossed around and bang her head before she could start that big adventure. But in the end, it was all worth it. You bought this book, so you believe it's worth it too. We've got time to prepare… and the Yellow Brick Road awaits.

Throughout my career, I've been passionate about guiding leaders and their teams to embrace the future and adapt to change. Historically, I've recognized possibilities earlier and chosen to face headwinds first, knowing the path was necessary. I've been privileged to be part of the extraordinary impact that transformation has had on organizations and I've lived long enough to see changes have an impact on society. In hindsight, I recognize it's because I have a high tolerance for *moving with change*. My life has definitely been richer for those experiences.

With this book, I'm encouraging leaders to move with change more easily by sharing stories of other successful leaders in this contemporary tale of a journey to the New Oz. I want you to experience the impact of leading teams to discover new paths, especially when it's messy and uncomfortable. And even beyond the workplace, wherever you've earned the respect of others, there's an opportunity to exercise the core values and skills in this book to ultimately prepare society for a more prosperous, innovative, and inclusive future.

As a champion for change, I know innovation and collaboration enable success. Leaders who support and embrace ambiguity are able to cultivate thriving teams capable of seizing new opportunities. With AI innovation

INTRODUCTION

progressing at breakneck speed, there's no better time for leaders to act and shape a future based on AI-enabled collaboration and growth.

I want you to shine as early adopters by proactively introducing generative AI into your organizations. You're the leaders who will define our shared future. Don't wait for a corporate mandate or for IT to implement an elaborate new system. The truth is, almost any organization can adopt individual or shared AI technology improvements. These changes enhance performance and fuel the learning process for your teams to embrace the possibilities of the new technology. By encouraging an early adoption mindset, we can forge a resilient new future that taps into AI's potential to revolutionize industries, enhance collaboration, and create a more sustainable, equitable world for everyone.

In AI *and the New Oz*, we'll share stories that demonstrate the difference leadership makes, with real-world examples that will help motivate you to take on the challenges of incorporating AI into your organization. By combining personal experiences and the collective wisdom of industry experts, we'll equip you with the insights and tools you'll need to lead your organization confidently and purposefully into the AI era. Together, we'll create a future that not only welcomes AI, but also nurtures a culture of innovation, collaboration, growth, and inclusion.

This is a Hands-On Assignment, *in every way*

GPT-4 was my writing and collaboration partner throughout this book, and frankly it made writing the book a little more difficult. GPT-4's voice and my voice competed for the mic on more than one occasion. Even so, collaborating with generative AI tools to write AI *and the New Oz* was a requirement that led to better conversations every time I gathered information.

It will be the same when leading teams through strategic change brought about by AI adoption. I'm all-in. Generative AI is already transformative, and we're just getting started. My assignment in this world is to dig deep and help people get ready for the big shifts our workforce and society will experience as a result of these changes. I can't do that from the skybox suites. I need to practice what I preach.

Generative AI is different from all the other technologies I've taken to market and implemented over the last 20+ years, because it's "everyman's" technology. GenAI is for the masses, so we all need to engage personally.
Each of us needs to develop our own point of view by understanding how these tools work and what we think can be accomplished with them.

I didn't have deep technical knowledge of most of the technology I delivered during the last 20 years; I didn't need it. That's because my role as a leader was to effectively scale organizations and resources, not to troubleshoot software code. GenAI is different, because it's so accessible. We cannot escape this new reality; it's applicable to every level of our work. Leaders who don't pay attention and who apply the old mindset to "let the teams figure it out" will find themselves unable to relate to discussions at Board meetings, in company All-Hands discussions, and even at the dinner table with their 9-year-old.

I could've joined my colleagues on the technical side who are debating the merits of security, access, ethics, bad actors, and regulatory guardrails. Very capable people are working on those issues, and I'm confident that solutions to those topics will take shape over the next year or two. It's worthwhile work, but it's not the best use of my skills or my heart. What needs attention today is those who are **not** moving toward AI adoption. I can help them focus on their plan — of their own free will, with their own ideas, thinking strategically about the future.

My goal is to get all leaders — big leaders, little leaders, tall leaders, small leaders, less-technical leaders, even not-yet leaders (those are my favorites!) — mobilized and moving to foundationally understand collective intelligence and take control of their future, now. Don't draw the curtains on your house and wait for the storm to blow past. I need you to open that curtain, take a good look at the coming tornado, and get ready for a wild ride.

We have the tools we need. (You already know what I'm going to say next...) **But technical tools aren't what these organizations need.** What these organizations need are leadership tools, change management tools, and cultural tools. We need to empower teams to create the answers to build the tools for their future.

You knew that already; it's why you bought this book. And we're going to break it down by section into useful practical things you can do to prepare yourself to lead through these challenging times and equip your teams to grow stronger.

Trail Markers for The Yellow Brick Road

To make AI and the New Oz more useful, I've included road signs to help us navigate AI's Yellow Brick Road. The journey may not always be clearly marked, but these should at least make your compass easier to use.

At the end of each chapter is a section titled "**AI Adoption Accelerators**" marked by a ROCKET SHIP. This information will offer best practices and ideas related to that chapter's theme that can be used now – without IT capital spend or a team of advisory firm consultants spending months

INTRODUCTION

learning your business. Some of these items are obvious and others are pretty creative. These 6-8 thought-starters per chapter are a starting point for you and your teams for low-overhead, stand-alone things you can start doing *right now*. Have fun with it.

I'm an experienced professional. Having said that, there will be times when I just can't help myself, and all my enthusiasm, passion, and experience is going to come right out of my fingers on this keyboard. When those **"Make a Difference"** moments happen, I want you to slow down and read carefully. It took me 25 years, a million miles on airplanes, a little self-doubt (we've all been there), and a lot of time focused on doing everything instead of the right things to recognize those moments were important to share, so you don't have to figure them out like I did. They're the better transformational learning moments in this book (or at the very least, they're "save you some pain and suffering" moments) and they'll be accessorized by Judy Garland's ICONIC RUBY RED SLIPPERS. Throw a little Southern flair on those sentences if you're feeling the moment with me.

As the book evolved, there were areas that emerged as important building blocks for the New Oz – so **"Build Your Future"** became a trail marker. I highlighted those with the WIZARD'S CASTLE to guide us when there's an opportunity to prepare ahead for what will be needed to secure and protect successful AI adoption in the future.

And now – let's take a quick overview of our road trip to the New Oz...

In the first chapter, we begin our journey on the Yellow Brick Road to AI Adoption. We'll map the route to successful AI integration and make plans to prevent future issues from arising on the journey by establishing clarity from the beginning. Preparation is key, and so is communication and team input.

As we continue our adventure, we discover that our beloved main characters possess the qualities that define extraordinary leaders in the New Oz. Dorothy takes center stage in Chapter 2, showcasing her talent for assembling teams. Her keen eye for talent enables her to unearth the innate gifts in people. Her ability to identify and nurture these talents creates a formidable team of unlikely peers. Many of us come to possess this ability when we take the time to truly see others, a crucial skill for success and thriving in the New Oz.

In Chapter 3, The Cowardly Lion's Bravery, we'll see what happens when a leader makes bold changes. Bravery and resilience isn't reserved only for leaders; these traits quickly spread to the teams who observe the impact of those actions, if you encourage and enable this.

The Tin Man joins our story in Chapter 4 to #LeadwithLove and offers real-world examples for recognizing the significance of compassion in the AI era to

INTRODUCTION

profoundly affect employees and customers. This goodwill permeates society, turning even the coldest hearts into compassionate leaders for good.

The Scarecrow's Quest for Wisdom in Chapter 5 emphasizes the importance of lifelong learning as leaders learn to strike a balance between technology and human intuition. I particularly adore the Scarecrow's story, because he was much smarter than he realized; he just needed someone to believe in him. We'll discuss this key to success in the New Oz in the context of recognizing our teams' value and how we can engage them through changing our business models, creating use cases, early training, and creating a learning culture within our teams.

In The Wizard's Vision in Chapter 6, we'll look at the story of a visionary thought leader who sees a world where AI and humans collaborate to solve intricate problems. Imagining and planning for a flourishing, AI-enabled world, and involving our teams in that process will alter the narrative of how well society adapts to the impending waves of change.

Of course, no one expects the path to AI adoption to be flawless or without challenge. The Wicked Witch of Resistance flies in for Chapter 7 where we examine the conflicts leaders face when implementing AI and how fostering a culture of innovation and adaptability is key to managing resistance.

In Chapter 8, we explore Collaboration as the antidote to conflict and resistance. This chapter showcases The Munchkin Land of Collaboration's power in engaging others to a common outcome and reveals the possible turnaround when different organizations and disciplines begin to work together. This chapter includes a cameo from the Flying Monkeys, who introduce examples for networking and building alliances.

As we bring this adventure full circle in Chapter 9, we already know **There's No Place Like Home**. Our future is what **we** make it ... and it begins right now. Let's take this exciting journey to New Oz together, where the magic of AI and leadership create a bright future brimming with innovation, collaboration, and growth.

Let the journey begin!

Chapter 1

THE YELLOW BRICK ROAD TO AI ADOPTION

"It's always best to start at the beginning. And all you do is follow the Yellow Brick Road." – Glinda the Good Witch

An Overnight Sensation... 80 Years in the Making

MANY BELIEVE THAT THE recent surge of AI activity stemming from ChatGPTs meteoric launch was an unexpected surge of technical innovation. Interest grew rapidly – so rapidly that some questioned its staying power. However, as Marc Andreessen noted in a recent essay,[4] the development of Artificial Intelligence actually started way back in the 1940s (simultaneous with the invention of the computer), and the first scientific paper on neural networks was published in 1943 (just four years after filming *The Wizard of Oz*).

As Andreessen poignantly noted, "Entire generations of AI scientists over the last 80 years were born, went to school, worked, and in many cases passed away without seeing the payoff that we are receiving now." By no means is this an overnight sensation. As they say in Music City USA – my hometown of Nashville, Tennessee – AI definitely isn't a "one-hit wonder."

The world is on the cusp of a transformation unlike any we've witnessed before. Artificial Intelligence will revolutionize industries and create possibilities beyond our wildest imaginations. It's a realm where **human intellect** and **machine ingenuity** will converge to drive progress and shape our collective future. That's an important point we shouldn't ignore: the **partnership** of human and machine is where we'll soon see innovation and growth that are very different than past results.

Throughout this journey, I'll sometimes use the term "collective intelligence" in lieu of "artificial intelligence." I borrowed the term from an essay written by Roen Prowe of Snow Creek Advisory about the convergence of intelligent systems – man and machine, culture and platform – enabling a future of personalization and capabilities that weren't previously possible.[5] I'm impressed how the term "collective intelligence" signifies the human contribution necessary for thriving in the man-machine collaboration we're currently navigating; the subtle undertones in the phrase are particularly compelling to me.

With the advancement that AI enables, the true catalyst for change lies beyond the algorithms. The catalyst exists within the leaders who champion AI adoption and empower teams to push the boundaries of what is possible. As these teams grow and connect with other teams, they'll create systems that elevate their productivity, delivery, knowledge, and contributions — effectively building the New Oz. We'll see wholesale shifts in society. And it all starts with leaders, elevating teams... connecting to more leaders, elevating more teams. It starts now, on the Yellow Brick Road.

Directions to the AI Trailhead

In my opinion, there are few pure technologists who exist at the level of Bill Gates. It's rare to see someone who maintained such acute technical vision and competency while building business acumen on a global scale *and* addressing broad societal issues like poverty, health, and education. Bill is a human unicorn. (Melinda, too. They're both shining beacons of how to transform countless lives by utilizing their hard-earned privilege for the greatest good.)

Bill now focuses a lot of his attention on pandemic prevention and battling worldwide poverty; his efforts are less about the flashy allure of cutting-edge tech than about fixing societal problems that predate the first computer. This fact makes his reaction in the *Gates Notes* blog post following GPT-4's unveiling, all the more remarkable:[6]

> **The development of AI is as fundamental as the creation of the microprocessor, the personal computer, the Internet, and the mobile phone.**
>
> It will change the way people **work, learn, travel, get health care, and communicate** with each other.
>
> **Entire industries will reorient around it.** Businesses will distinguish themselves by how well they use it.
>
> **BILL GATES**

Google's Sundar Pichai famously said AI is "more profound than fire or electricity."[7] And now Bill's in the mix with the personal computer, the internet, *and* the mobile phone — *these guys are not messing around!* They're Pathfinders. They deliver consistent messages, not about their current and former technology companies, but about the potential for AI to have a meaningful impact on how we live, work, and engage as humanity. That's far bigger than any single product or company.

So is it possible we've been on this journey all along? Andreessen pointed out AI has been under development since the 1940s, Sundar says it's as profound as fire, and Bill Gates is talking about AI being as fundamental as PCs and cell phones. These things have all been around... well, for a long time. [Some of you just had your "ah-ha" moment; but don't put the book down... stay with me here.] Yes, it does seem this has been in process for a bit. Here's my story; see if you can relate (if you're a GenX'er, you may relate faster):

- I was 11 years old (the same age as Dorothy Gale in *The Wizard of Oz*) when I got my first **personal computer** – a Commodore Vic-20, and I barely knew what to do with it. It was an 8-bit system with enough RAM to manage half of a sheet of typed text.

- **You've Got Mail!** Ten years after that Vic-20, I bought my first Macintosh Classic. Around that time, the glory days of AOL dial-up internet service screeeeched into our lives in 1991.[5] Remember the dial-up connection tone? My cat hid under the bed every time my modem connected – which was a lot

THE YELLOW BRICK ROAD TO AI ADOPTION   19

(unfortunately for the cat).

- **And the "mobile" phone.** I was at dinner with grad school classmates when we saw our first cell phone "in the wild" – an 8-pound "brick" with a 12-inch antenna. It would be well over a decade of suffering through good intentions before the first iPhone hit the market in 2007.[6]

Graduating from the Vic-20 to the iPhone took 27 years. The technologies are largely unrelated, but society's evolution of communication, opportunity, and even prosperity sit virtually on the same continuum. As these fundamental technologies were launched – the personal computer in the early 80s, home internet in the early 90s, and the mobile telephone in the 2000s – depending on your situation, everything from the buying process to the price of the new tech to the skills needed to use it were all potential barriers to entry.

That Vic-20 may seem absurdly primitive now, but my parents sacrificed to scrape together the money to put that computer under the Christmas tree. Home internet access and mobile phones were only easily available to me because I worked for Tech companies and those were necessary job tools. Early in the adoption cycle for those technologies, access was often limited by geography, financial priority, or technical familiarity.

But things have certainly changed.

Fast-forward 20 years (okay, 30 years). The world is far more technologically sophisticated. Groceries and fast food can be delivered to our doorstep, on pre-scheduled intervals if desired. Toddlers routinely pick up iPads and FaceTime their grandparents. It's a different world entirely. But people were still caught off guard when ChatGPT launched on November 30, 2022 and this happened:

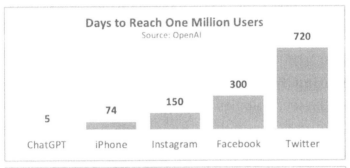

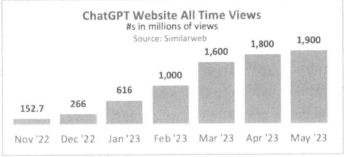

In five days, OpenAI reached a million users with the ChatGPT product. (Other well-known platforms took between two months and two years to reach a million users.) And usage? May saw just short of two billion site views.[10]

How? Easy – there were no real barriers to entry; you only needed to be curious. We didn't need to build roads or cities. Steam plants didn't have to be constructed and electrical lines didn't have to be run to deliver power to consumers. We already had the equipment to use it (literally, in our back pockets). We only needed an internet connection and curiosity.

No barriers = 1 million users in 5 days. The user count reached 173 million users in April 2023[11] and the appetite for creativity and growth that has been unleashed is like nothing most of us have experienced. It's sort of startling for those of us who lived through so many incremental changes.

Does Volume = Traction?

My own journey with ChatGPT didn't start until well after the holidays. I started writing this book in March, largely because so many of my colleagues weren't engaging with it (and the majority of those people work in or adjacent to the Tech sector). It's now May, I'm writing the final chapters of AI *and the New* Oz, and I'm conflicted with two thoughts:

1. **I'm amazed by the velocity.** Records broken for new users at every turn. Approximately six *hundred* new AI tools delivered weekly to market. I haven't gone to bed before midnight since this odyssey began – it's an absolute frenzy. It feels like I'm in the middle of a cyclone of activity, and I'm not sure where it will put me down.

2. **I'm bewildered by the ambivalence.** I speak with well-informed, forward-thinking professionals almost daily. These leaders carry immense responsibilities and acknowledge that AI is revolutionizing our world, yet they haven't used a

single generative AI tool created in the past six months, nor do they plan to do so.

Companies are behaving similarly. A KPMG survey of enterprise executives[9] revealed that 60% are still "a year or two away" from implementing their **first** generative AI solution. 68% haven't even appointed a central person or team to organize their response to the emergence of GenAI; only 6% have a dedicated team to handle risks as part of their overall generative AI strategy (although "risks" is one of two primary barriers to progress cited by the survey).

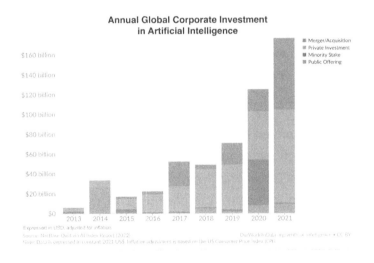

It appears that innovation delivery is far outpacing demand. Overall global corporate investment in broader artificial intelligence has been growing for almost a decade (see graphic). In 2013, we barely invested $10B in AI; compare this to well over $160B of corporate investment in 2021. With the recent advances in large language models,

Venture Capitalists have steadily increased their positions in generative AI, funding four times more in the first half of 2023 the amount that was funded in all of 2022: $12.7 billion in the first five months of 2023, compared with $4.8 billion in all of 2022 for VC funding of generative AI startups, according to PitchBook.[13] Angel and seed deals have also grown, with 107 deals and $358.3 million invested in 2022 compared with just 41 and $102.8 million in 2018.[14] At least 36 generative AI companies have raised $100M in funding as of June 2023.[15]

We're innovating with hundreds of new AI-enabled tools and products per week, but people and teams are reluctant to explore them. In a Hunter Marketing survey of 300 executives,[16] 68% of leaders not using AI were concerned about the ethical use of the technology, and nearly half of the executives not using AI (45%) feel it is not accurate enough yet. Business executives who don't use AI also indicated it is not in their scope and is owned by the IT department (72%), and the benefits of using AI aren't clear to them (62%).

In the same Hunter Marketing survey, executives were asked what resources and support they wanted their companies to provide to help them use AI. Respondents from the C-Suite offered these insights:

- 58% wanted AI tools implemented to help them do their job

- 55% wanted to work on a project to help their company adopt AI

- 55% wanted their company to offer internal education on AI

- 47% wanted their company to set guidelines on what they can and can't do related to AI

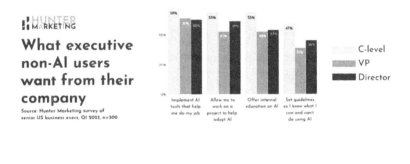

Why I Wrote The New Oz

It is blatantly obvious that many industries are hesitating. Leaders are the answer, but they're not engaging.

It's up to Leadership to usher AI forward. Every situation will be different and every company's journey is unique. In many respects, AI is stalled at the adoption and implementation phases because leaders aren't clear how to proceed – the transformative potential is too significant, and they don't have a roadmap. The map will evolve; they need to start walking. With the latest shifts in technology, those decisions can and will occur at the ground level. Leaders across all functions will lead this – we can, and we must. As an admired colleague has a habit of saying, "It's work, but it's worthy."[17]

Route Planning for the Yellow Brick Road

In the timeless tale of *The Wizard of Oz*, the Yellow Brick Road isn't just a simple path to reach the Emerald City. The journey is a story filled with side-plots, surprises, challenges, and rewards. The road to AI adoption is no different. It requires meticulous planning, buy-in from all participants, and a robust governance structure. This is where our journey begins.

First, like Dorothy, we must recognize that we're absolutely not in Kansas anymore. The world around us is morphing at a speed we would never have imagined and AI is an integral part of the transformation. The first step in our journey, then, is acceptance – acceptance that to remain competitive and relevant, we must adapt and change. That cyclone has brought us to a whole new world in record time.

The next phase is planning. Dorothy didn't step onto the Yellow Brick Road without preparing. She had her basket, her dog Toto, and a firm resolve to meet the Wizard. Just as Dorothy had to prepare herself for the journey, we also need to gather our resources, assemble our team, and map our route.

At the beginning of your planning phase, you need to clearly define your objectives. AI is astounding, but it's still a tool. What do you hope to achieve with AI? Is it a drastic improvement in operational efficiency? Is it about enhancing customer experiences? Or is it about breaking barriers to create novel products and services? Defining where you want to go gives your journey direction and purpose.

Once your objectives are set, it's time to identify your stakeholders. These people will directly or indirectly influence or be influenced by your AI initiatives. They could be your employees, customers, investors, or maybe even industry regulators. It's crucial to get their buy-in early, as they will be your companions along the Yellow Brick Road.

Next, take stock of your resources. What skills do you currently have in-house? What new capabilities will you need to develop or acquire? Dorothy didn't have much to start with, and you may not either. That doesn't mean you can't get started, as long as you're honest about what you have and don't have. Examine your existing infrastructure and determine what needs to be upgraded or replaced. The answers to these questions form the foundation of your AI initiatives.

Then, develop a governance structure. As we travel the Yellow Brick Road, we'll encounter many decisions – some routine, others strategic. Who's going to make these decisions? How will they be made? These are questions your governance structure must anticipate. Furthermore, identify potential risks and challenges and how to mitigate them. It wasn't smooth sailing for Dorothy — she tackled the Wicked Witch of the West and had to outsmart those flying monkeys! Your journey will also have its fair share of obstacles. Anticipating them allows you to prepare and respond effectively.

Lastly, define your success metrics — the milestones that will guide you and help you stay on track. The Yellow Brick Road is long and winding, and it's easy to get lost or distracted. Success metrics provide clarity and focus, ensuring you and the teams are always moving toward your goal. If you know where you're going, you'll know when you get there.

Additional Preparation for the Long & Winding (Yellow Brick) Road

There's no formula-driven answer for how to build an AI strategy. It always depends on your company's offerings, pain points, size/distribution/maturity, appetite for change, and what you need to accomplish. There are good business practices that would be the wrong direction in some companies, and the opposite can also be true. There are, however, a few basic considerations worth committing to ink. Many of the following concepts have been around longer than I've been in the workforce and there is ample high-quality documentation to support them. Most of these are, by now, common wisdom, but they remain challenges because we haven't prioritized them or had the discipline to commit to action on a routine basis. It's never too late to start!

Research the latest planning trends and models in AI. If your company has a business maturity model or planning framework, use that as a potential baseline for where your organization sits on the implementation journey. If you don't have a model to work with, it's a worthwhile 20-minute exercise to find a few online and explore where you might fit. Search for "AI Maturity Model" and enjoy exploring what other companies position as growth opportunities and how consulting firms measure their clients.

As you consider and prioritize where to invest time on AI initiatives, it's useful to see where other companies are spending their time. There's a time and place to be first in innovation; there's also something to be said for leveraging known territory and producing a win with your teams. If you're relatively new in the AI adoption cycle, my heartfelt suggestion would be to take an easy win and demonstrate **value** to your team. There's plenty of time to set the world on fire with new creative energy after you've convinced your teams about the magic AI will bring with the early projects you implement.

Develop a point of view about how AI will enable your business. One of the best visuals I've seen to describe the change in delivery models AI will enable in the New Oz was created by Jamie Peebles, a LinkedIn connection, company founder, and AI thought leader. He created the visuals below to show how AI will likely augment our capabilities, freeing us from repetitive tasks, and enabling us to focus on higher-value services.[18] The Current State graphic is easy enough to understand – we receive information and then process any number of tasks required to compile or complete the necessary deliverable.

In the Future State graphic, Peebles suggests there will be significant potential for several of our current tasks to be completed in partnership with us and AI, or for some of our current tasks to be handled entirely by AI. Not only does AI manage many tasks for us (or in partnership with us), but notice how it also presents an opportunity to take on completely new tasks. These new tasks (also handled either by AI or in partnership with AI) represent a line of new activity — that's new "Value," whether it's revenue generation or just competitive value-add. The "branches" of activity at the far right end of the graphic represent the new and additional activity that should be possible when the linear work from the Current State (above) is AI-enabled in the future (below).

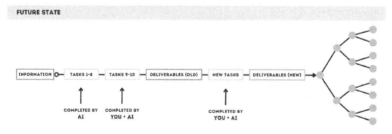

Peebles' real-world example of this was the introduction of QuickBooks software. QuickBooks automated manual activities formerly handled by accountants and bookkeepers, but those professionals weren't replaced by the software. Instead, they continued to thrive by using the new software automations and building on new value-added services like long-term planning, forecasting, and even QuickBooks setup. The reduction of hands-on activity leads to business considerations around price compression, workforce planning, and how to help businesses be more operational, strategic, and data-driven. As with any change, the transition may be challenging, but the key is to adapt and find new ways to deliver value.

Another forward-thinking LinkedIn connection, Stephanie Schwab, is the Founder & CEO of Crackerjack Marketing. Aligned to Jamie Peebles' concept above, Stephanie sings the praises of AI radically improving how her business operates in just the first half of this year: more organized, more time for creativity, ahead of the editorial calendar.[19] Many thought marketing agencies would close when generative AI first came on the scene. People like Stephanie chose to make AI a partner in optimizing her business to do more, build it smarter, deliver it better.

Identify Potential Value-Add Use Cases. Once you've identified ways that AI can impact your workflows and processes, it may be useful to see whether and how

THE YELLOW BRICK ROAD TO AI ADOPTION   31

your analysis aligns with efforts underway at other organizations. The sample below is an excerpt from a December 2022 report from McKinsey & Company that shows the most popular use cases their customers are implementing.[20] You can find this type of information online from most of the major advisory firms. Just search "AI Use Cases," and you'll be flooded with ideas by industry, vertical, and function; it's endless, and a great way to research various routes for your initial efforts, tailored to your particular priorities.

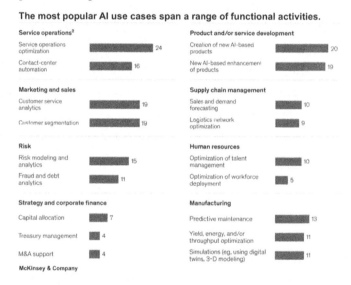

Vision → Strategy → Plan. This is almost a "mantra" in the corporate lexicon. These mechanical "specs" of execution are critical. Dorothy didn't have much when she started down that yellow brick road, but she did have a vision of what she wanted. Don't consider leaving on this expedition without a well-thought-out set of at least the Vision and Strategy of your AI-related business needs. In these hyper-dynamic times, finely detailed plans may be impractical, and adaptability is increasingly important. Team members need to adjust as plans are fine-tuned with new technological advances, business models, and customer requirements.

Get your Data "house" in order. This requirement is not going away. Data governance and data management continue to be significant impediments to progress at the corporate level with 77% of data practitioners reporting data quality issues.[21] One recent report warned that organizations have increasingly moved to a decentralized data model, with 43% currently using an average of 4-6 data platforms.[22] This data sprawl, among other complexities, makes it more difficult to maintain good data hygiene, consistency, and usage, making any cross-functional platform-level AI deployment challenging to manage consistently across functions, regions, products, etc.

It's up to leaders to seize this moment and guide our teams toward a brighter tomorrow. We're the Torchbearers who will illuminate the path forward, inspiring our organizations to embrace the possibilities of AI and chart a course toward progress, innovation, and success. Together, we'll change the world and create a legacy that will endure for generations to come.

As we prepare for this journey, we need to remember the lessons from our friends in Oz. Dorothy couldn't get to her destination on her own, and neither can we. Just as Dorothy won the buy-in of the Scarecrow, Tin Man, and Lion, we must also win the support of our stakeholders. As the Scarecrow valued intelligence, we need to value data and insights in our decision-making. As the Tin Man yearned for a heart, we must ensure our AI initiatives are ethical and beneficial for all. And as the Lion understood the need for courage, we must have the courage to venture into this new realm, face challenges, and embrace opportunities.

And what about the Wizard? Don't underestimate the value he created as the visionary leader. As leaders, we'll all cast our vision for AI as we inspire and guide our teams toward the New Oz. You're a role model, period. People will be looking to your insights and responses to inform their opinions and determine their level of commitment and engagement. Modeling positivity and gratitude in an authentic way influences teams to be of similar minds. That outlook in a team doesn't hide or erase challenges; it just makes the challenges easier to navigate.

The Yellow Brick Road to AI Adoption isn't just about implementing a new technology; it's about undertaking a transformational journey. Like all great journeys, it begins with a single, purposeful step. The time for action has arrived. The house has landed, those ruby red slippers are on our feet, and I do believe that pathway is turning more yellow by the minute.

Oz is waiting.

AI Adoption ACCELERATORS

The items below are elements of the toolkit for guiding an organization through an important change, whether it's a company of thousands or a team small enough to feed with a couple of pizzas. These are the foundations of the Yellow Brick Road, though company culture and size will often influence the level of formality involved in the deliverables. It's okay if your team is less directly involved in decisions about broader initiatives at your company – but **don't ever wait for someone else to tell you what's important to your business.**

Go ahead and start now — where you are, with what you have. Trust me: no one will ever fault you for making progress within your own areas of responsibility.

AI READINESS ASSESSMENT

- Evaluate your team's current capabilities, strengths, and opportunities for growth.

- Identify specific areas where AI can add value and improve processes.

- Also evaluate your team's current understanding, attitudes, and concerns about AI technology to identify potential areas of resistance so you can

THE YELLOW BRICK ROAD TO AI ADOPTION 35

tailor your approach accordingly. Even the best tools won't do you any good if your people can't or won't use them.

AI USE CASES

- Collaborate with your team to pinpoint high-impact AI applications that align with your organization's objectives and have the potential to generate significant value.

- Take the initiative to have your teams begin optimizing their work practices now.

AI-FOCUSED COMMUNICATION PLAN

- Develop a clear and consistent communication strategy to keep your team informed about AI initiatives, progress, and successes. Foster a sense of ownership and commitment to the vision.

- In particular, make sure you communicate the goals, benefits, and expected outcomes of AI adoption to your team.

- For fun, engage team members to use new AI tools to deliver various parts of the communication plan.

- Address misconceptions or fears and be transparent about the impact on roles and responsibilities. Things will change, and your people need to be ready for that. Consistent and open communication will build trust and help reduce resistance.

AI INTEGRATION STRATEGY & ADOPTION ROADMAP

- Create a detailed plan outlining the timelines, milestones, and necessary resources for successful AI integration, ensuring your team has a shared understanding of the objectives and steps involved. Make sure you anticipate potential roadblocks and factor them in.

- No matter what your title is, **it's your job** to present the AI roadmap to your team. The AI adoption journey is every leader's responsibility, not just IT or Corporate Strategy. When you own the message for your team (in partnership or in addition to other groups), **your group** will be successful.

  Personally deliver the message to your teams and field their questions (don't worry if you need to get answers and circle back). Try it – I promise it will transform your team, and you.

- Address common concerns and questions by compiling a comprehensive and accessible FAQ document that provides clarity and reassurance to the team. Make sure this resource is a dynamic one, growing along with your understanding of and experience with AI.

AI SUGGESTION BOX

- Set up a channel for team members to submit ideas, feedback, and concerns regarding AI adoption.

- Your team's voices are valued; show them how feedback is incorporated into the decision-making process.

PERFORMANCE METRICS

- Define specific, measurable goals related to AI adoption that can be tracked and assessed over time.

- Determine how to make AI metrics transparent across the organization (like all important team metrics).

- Cover progress on AI-related goals at an organizational level on at least a monthly basis.

Chapter 2

DOROTHY'S EYE FOR TALENT

"Lions and tigers and bears! Oh my!" – Dorothy

WE CAN'T VENTURE TOO far along the Yellow Brick Road without feeling the presence of Dorothy Gale – the heart of our story, an ordinary farm girl from Kansas who demonstrated an exceptional knack for assembling talent and bringing together the A-team that faced and overcame challenges on their journey to the Emerald City.

Dorothy's Leadership Style

Much like the successful integration of AI technologies will be, Dorothy's journey wasn't a solo effort; it involved an epic blending of skills, experiences, perspectives, and talents. She traveled to the Emerald City with a Tin Man with no heart, a Scarecrow with no brain, and a Lion with no courage. Many outside observers would have declared the group an odd mix, but we know each member was instrumental to the team's success and contributed unique skills that guided their journey through Oz.

Dorothy's inclusive leadership style in *The Wizard of Oz* helped her build a diverse team that achieved results because of her empathy, emotional intelligence, and adaptability. Her companions were unconventional, but she listened to their stories and understood their needs, fostering a sense of trust and belonging within the group.

Dorothy's leadership was built on mutual respect and collaboration, enabling her team to overcome the various obstacles they encountered on their way to the Emerald City. She had an open mind and heart that allowed her to see the potential in her mismatched companions. Despite their differences and perceived weaknesses, Dorothy embraced them and brought out their best. She inspired the Scarecrow to think, the Tin Man to feel, and the Cowardly Lion to be brave.

Dorothy created a sense of belonging and unity among her team members, who were diverse and had distinct abilities – abilities they didn't know they had. Her ability to identify and leverage her teammates' strengths while being sensitive to their limitations and insecurities strengthened her influence. She built genuine connections with each of her team members and leveraged the strength of those relationships to build their confidence in their own talents and skills.

By valuing the individuality and differences within her team, Dorothy created an inclusive environment that fostered collaboration and mutual support. Consequently, she was able to inspire and create momentum within her team, ultimately leading them to achieve their goals successfully.

Inclusive Leadership in AI Adoption

Similar to Dorothy's approach, as leaders in the New Oz we need to foster an environment that encourages diversity, inclusivity, and innovation. As AI technologies continue to transform the workplace, leaders will need to adapt and create a culture that embraces change and experimentation. A diverse team with a range of perspectives, skills, and experiences will be better equipped to navigate the complexities of AI and generate creative solutions when challenges arise.

Promoting transparency and open communication about AI technologies will be very important, as will addressing concerns and dispelling misconceptions to build trust and encourage employees to explore AI's potential. Remember that AI's customer is always a human. To achieve this partnership, leaders must involve their teams in AI scoping and development, ensuring that human values and needs remain firmly at the core of AI systems.

Dorothy's "Zones of Genius" for AI Leaders

Dorothy's story is a powerful metaphor for inclusive leadership in the era of AI adoption. She approached each new companion with an open mind and a willingness to listen. By learning from her ability to create an inclusive environment and form a diverse team, leaders can successfully navigate the complexities and unknowns of AI.

Dorothy's "zones of genius" below would serve us well as we travel our own Yellow Brick Road with teams who deserve our whole-hearted leadership.

Encourage experimentation and learning: Embracing the complexities and unknowns of AI technology will require leaders to adopt a similar openness and adaptability to Dorothy's leadership style. As AI continues to evolve, leaders will need to be agile and open to change, guiding their teams through the uncertainties and challenges of AI adoption. Leaders need to actively encourage a culture of continuous learning and collaboration to ensure employees have the necessary skills and knowledge to navigate the rapidly changing AI landscape.

Embrace diversity: A key aspect of Dorothy's leadership was her ability to create an inclusive environment that recognized the value of each team member's unique abilities. This is essential for AI adoption because diverse perspectives and skills are critical in unlocking the full potential of AI technologies. By promoting inclusivity, leaders create an environment that encourages creativity, innovation, and collaboration, ultimately driving successful AI integration.

Recognize and nurture talent: Leaders will need to adopt a forward-thinking approach, anticipating the challenges and opportunities brought by AI. Actively working to identify and leverage the strengths within their teams will present opportunities to further develop skills within the group. AI will drive significant changes in the workforce; some roles will become obsolete, and new roles will emerge. Adapting to these changes will require leaders to be proactive in recognizing and developing the new skills and abilities needed for success in an AI-driven world. This requires a keen eye for talent and the ability to identify and nurture the skills and abilities needed for success in the AI-enabled future.

Richard Branson's Talent Focus

Dorothy is an impactful example of what can happen when a leader sees the unexpected talent in team members and nurtures that for the greater good. In the modern world, there's an iconic figure whose leadership style resembles Dorothy's. He built his own Emerald City in the business realm, carving out a significant niche in multiple industries, including music, travel, and space. Richard Branson – the flamboyant billionaire and founder of the Virgin Group with a knack for assembling talent and nurturing diversity – echoes Dorothy's own team-building aptitude (on a somewhat larger scale).

Branson is well-known for his keen ability to assemble talented, diverse teams. Vanderbilt University professor Jane Robbins notes that he has built his brand by employing people he can involve in the process; it reveals how central employees are to Branson's success.[23] Branson's quote below is one of many showing how seriously he takes his role as a leader who prioritizes nurturing teams to do great things (so he can go do other new great things).

> Having a personality of caring about people is important. You can't be a good leader unless you generally like people. That is how you bring out the best in them.[24] A company is people... employees want to know... am I being listened to or am I a cog in the wheel? People really need to feel wanted.[25]

Like Dorothy and her diverse companions, Branson saw beyond the external or obvious and understood the value that unique perspectives and skills would bring to his team. A significant part of the Oz narrative is Dorothy enabling the Tin Man, the Scarecrow, and the Lion to recognize and harness their own unique strengths. Branson has always been adept at identifying and nurturing hidden talents within his teams. He has consistently empowered people and given them the opportunity to shine, fostering an environment where innovation thrives and guides them to remarkable goals.

This innate ability to rally a diverse group of people around a shared vision, to empower them and foster an environment of mutual respect and collaboration, is what sets both Dorothy and Branson apart. In this era of AI adoption, leaders should strive to emulate these qualities to successfully shepherd their teams through the transition.

Integrating AI into everyday life will be as monumental and challenging as journeying to the Emerald City. It demands a great deal of courage, intelligence, and heart and requires leaders who can inspire trust, foster collaboration, and maintain a clear vision for the future.

Branson's Success Empowering Diverse Teams

In Branson's autobiography, *Finding My Virginity*, he reflects on instances where he gathered people from diverse backgrounds to launch or save his ventures. Leaders who want a successful AI journey should consider doing the same and prioritize building teams with a broad range of skills and backgrounds. Just like Dorothy and her friends, each member of the team brings something unique to the table – whether it's courage to venture into unknown territory, the heart to understand and empathize with those affected by changes, or the brains to design and implement unique processes and AI systems. And remember – she didn't know ahead of time what skills those team members would bring, but was ready and willing to embrace them and leverage them when they came along.

Branson's leadership philosophy is centered on taking care of his employees and empowering them to take care of his customers. His people-first approach resonates in the New Oz because successful AI adoption isn't just about implementing cutting-edge technology. It's about ensuring the technology serves us, makes our lives easier, and uplifts humanity. Keep in mind that the magic ruby slippers were a marvel, but they needed Dorothy to wear and use them.

Dorothy's journey and Branson's leadership philosophy remind us that an effective leader, like a wise conductor, brings out the best in each individual and harmonizes their talents to achieve a shared vision. In the evolving AI landscape leaders need to be more than tech-savvy; they also need strong focus to create a diverse, inclusive, and empowered team that navigates the challenges and opportunities that come with change.

In our journey to the New Oz, let's use the lessons learned from Dorothy and Richard Branson about the value of diversity and the power of an inclusive team. Let's celebrate the unique skills and perspectives each member brings as we make our way toward the Emerald City.

Together, we'll do more than just reach the New Oz. We'll also ensure it's a place that serves all of humanity as a true testament to the power of AI to enable our world to transform.

The story is – and it has always been – about the journey and the people we meet along the way. So let's boldly step forward, with the same courage, intelligence, and heart that guided Dorothy Gale and Richard Branson.

It's your journey. Make it magical.

DOROTHY'S EYE FOR TALENT

AI Adoption ACCELERATORS

Dorothy's unique ability to recognize and bring out the best in her diverse group of friends reflects the essential leadership skill of identifying and nurturing individual talents to create a strong team. By seeing beyond the surface and acknowledging the potential within each team member, leaders can assemble a powerful and cohesive unit capable of tackling the challenges of AI adoption. Exceptional leaders like Dorothy can foster an inclusive environment where everyone's unique strengths are harnessed, creating synergy that propels the team toward AI success. These ideas may help accelerate your current talent pool while you work toward AI adoption.

SKILLS INVENTORY

- Know what skills are on your team (both formal and informal). Assess the expertise within your team and identify areas of strength and opportunities for growth related to both short and long-term AI needs you're likely to experience.

- Make your own plan to grow your people specific to AI – and engage them in creating the plan.

DIVERSE PROJECT TEAMS & COMMUNICATION

- Form teams for AI projects and intentionally include a mix of backgrounds, skill sets, and perspectives to foster innovation and ensure that all voices are represented. Form a team this week – it might just be a brainstorming team, but get started.

- Use a variety of communication methods (written, verbal, and visual) to ensure all team members can effectively engage with AI-related information and discussions.

JOB ROTATIONS

- Allow team members to experience different roles within AI projects. Make this part of your plan and get input from your team. You don't know yet who's the best fit where, and neither do they. But you can figure it out together.

- Encourage your teams to be involved and have a well-rounded understanding of the technology and its applications. Invite people who may be interested and you'll be surprised who signs up.

INCLUSIVE CULTURE

- You really are the role model people watch, so create an environment where every team member feels valued and respected. It's important to make time for this – we're all busy and short-staffed, but it gets worse if you don't model behavior that encourages people to stick around. People are our priority, so make the time for them.

LEADERSHIP LAB & COACHING

- Create a dedicated space or program for team members to experiment with different leadership roles and responsibilities in a low-stakes environment. Include small-scale projects, problem-solving exercises, or simulations, that allow individuals to test their leadership skills and receive constructive feedback from peers and mentors.

- Use GPT-4 as a business coach to help your team members experience real-time collaboration for problem-solving, communications challenges, brainstorming, or development coaching. Just chat with GPT-4 to create an entire plan around marketing and launch of the coaching opportunity for your team.

Chapter 3

THE COWARDLY LION'S BRAVERY

"All you need is confidence in yourself. There is no living thing that is not afraid when it faces danger. The true courage is in facing danger when you are afraid, and that kind of courage you have in plenty." – The Wizard of Oz

THE COWARDLY LION WAS afraid of absolutely everything – afraid of the dark, afraid of heights, afraid of being alone – but when he met Dorothy and the others, he realized he actually had the courage to face his fears. With their help, he learned to stand up for himself and fight for what he believed in.

The Cowardly Lion's bravery was hidden by his timidity. When he faced the challenges of their journey through Oz and stood up to adversity, he found his true strength. His journey symbolizes the determination leaders and our teams will need as we navigate the uncertainty of redefining the future of work in the New Oz.

Leadership Courage

Leadership courage is the ability to make difficult decisions, *even when you're afraid*. It's the ability to stand up for what you believe in, *even when it's unpopular*. It's the ability to take risks, *even when you might fail*. Leaders who fear the prospects of change or become paralyzed by concerns about missteps may find themselves at an impasse when faced with the road to AI adoption. As Brené Brown points out, "We can choose courage or we can choose comfort, but we can't have both. Not at the same time."[26] The thing is, you really do get accustomed to living in the mode of "courage" instead of comfort when you're a leader. As leaders, we're constantly delivering change and growth, which is particularly relevant for AI adoption.

Choosing courage for AI adoption means embracing the changes made possible by technology shifts, understanding the implications, and working with them to create a more efficient, informed, and connected society. Comfort, on the other hand, means sticking to traditional, less-advanced methods. What if Netflix had stuck with "Comfort"? They might still be dispensing DVDs out of vending machines and we might never have streamed *Squid Game* or *Stranger Things*. (Or they might not even be in business anymore.)

Embracing AI can be scary because it often requires a shift in mindset, acquiring new skills, and a willingness to adapt. However, choosing courage over comfort means making this leap and harnessing the potential of AI, which can lead to significant progress and innovation in virtually every area of life and business. Note that choosing courage over comfort doesn't necessarily mean dismissing all fears and concerns. It means acknowledging those fears, and then making informed decisions about how to move forward despite them. It's about recognizing the potential benefits that outweigh the comfort of maintaining the status quo. Even after finding his inner courage, the Lion was still nervous when facing challenges – but now he faced them instead of running away.

Leadership courage is table-stakes in the dynamic world of AI adoption. Generative AI is a new and disruptive technology, and it can be difficult to know how to adopt it effectively. There are many risks associated with GenAI, so it's easy to get consumed by the possibility of making mistakes. Let me save you some time: you'll make a few. Everyone does. But leadership courage helps us overcome these fears and embrace AI as a tool for growth and innovation.

Accepting the Risk of Failure

From my vantage point, the general populace is only seven months into this generative AI exploration and the trajectory is anything but predictable. We're trailblazers in unexplored terrain, like the Cowardly Lion who summoned his courage in the face of fear. As leaders, we'll need to emulate the Lion's bravery when confronted with skepticism and resistance. Our journey to the New Oz will require us to face the unknown, risk failure, and accept the inevitable sea change this challenge brings.

The ability to take the risk of failure and make difficult choices is the hallmark of leadership courage. Leaders with fortitude champion their beliefs, even if they swim against the current of popular opinion. And like Dorothy, they bear the unique power to inspire others to join them on this journey, even when the path ahead is unclear.

The importance of courage in leadership cannot be understated. It's the firm guiding hand navigating leaders through treacherous decisions, the unwavering voice of resolve, and the driver of audacious risk-taking. A courageous leader doesn't just inspire; they radiate a contagious bravery that permeates their team. This bravery incubates innovation, accelerates growth, and cultivates an empowering, positive work environment.

Bold Moves to Accelerate an Industry

I met Troy at Peet's coffee shop just after GPT-4 launched.[27] He was one of the GMs I partnered with when I moved to California and remains one of my favorite Tech storytellers. Given the timing, there was an absolute frenzy of activity and creativity in our professional circles and we had plenty to discuss as we spoke about the bold courage leaders would need to navigate the future. I had just started drafting this book and knew he'd have a piece of history to connect with today's journey to the New Oz.

Troy spoke about his time working with John Chambers when Cisco pivoted its business model. John took a legendary risk that changed an industry and catapulted more than just Cisco. That pivot took courage, and the effects of that courage were amplified beyond a single company. This is likely to be our experience with AI.

John Chambers' story of courage began when he took the helm at Cisco in 1995. At the time, the company was known primarily for its multi-protocol routers, but Chambers quickly recognized that the future of networking actually lay in the emerging technologies of Internet Protocol (IP) and Ethernet. Despite the potential risks and uncertainties, he forged ahead with a major shift in strategy and steered Cisco to new horizons... and uncertain territory.

Chambers transformed Cisco from a multi-point network router company to a single TCP/IP configuration-focused company. At the time, IP and Ethernet technologies were gaining momentum because they offered cost-effective and scalable solutions for data communication networks. Under his leadership, Cisco acquired several companies specializing in IP and Ethernet technologies early on and rapidly expanded the product portfolio to solidify their market position.[28]

Driven by Chambers' courage and vision, the bold move paid off and the strategic shift had a massive impact on both Cisco and the technology industry as a whole. Cisco's focus on IP and Ethernet enabled them to capitalize on the growing demand for these technologies, leading to exponential growth in revenue and market share. Cisco became the world's largest provider of networking equipment with a dominant position in the IP and Ethernet markets.

Similar to our current-day AI challenge, Cisco's strategic move required immense courage at the beginning because it was a departure from the company's original path and involved entering unfamiliar territory. It's easy to say now that it was smart to invest in IP and Ethernet, but that wasn't at all obvious in 1995. The leap of faith Chambers took transformed the future of Cisco and is a powerful example of the courageous leadership needed for successful AI adoption.

Leadership Courage Inspires Others

Leadership courage is more than just making bold decisions. When done well, it inspires others to follow you. Courageous leaders create a sense of excitement and possibility. They help people see the potential to achieve great things and believe the risk will be worth the effort.

There was another important outcome with Cisco's bravery that was less obvious: *Cisco did not rise alone.* Troy explained that thousands of enterprise customers made a leap of faith along with Cisco. The people at the customer companies who made the jump also made huge leaps in their personal careers. When Cisco won, they won. It was risky to abandon a successful business model – and those who took the risk and made the effort were placing their bets on an unproven, nascent technology. Fifteen years later, those risk-takers were the leaders of industry throughout Silicon Valley.

Ethical Responsibility, Bias, and Courage

I'll make a bold prediction here. Leaders with strong courage are in need for this journey to the New Oz. But those who stand out will particularly be brave (and clear) in areas of social consciousness. Ethical responsibility in the delivery and application of GenAI is a growing area of focus as more employees use AI tools in the workplace. As adoption accelerates, leaders have an obligation to ensure these technologies are used responsibly and fairly. This means being vigilant about the potential biases and ethical implications of AI and actively working to mitigate these risks. By championing transparency, fairness, and inclusivity, leaders can build trust and cultivate a culture of responsible AI adoption that benefits all stakeholders and society as a whole.

Marko Jak is a Croatian-born Co-Founder in the AI consumer space. I've had the pleasure of working with his company's early launch efforts. Marko cares deeply about design principles and recently introduced me to the guiding principle below from *Hackers & Painters*,[29] a collection of essays by Y Combinator founder Paul Graham.

> You're most likely to get good design if the intended users include the designer himself. When you design something for a group that doesn't include you, it tends to be for people you consider less sophisticated than you, not more sophisticated. And looking down on the user, however benevolently, always seems to corrupt the designer. I suspect few housing projects in the US were

The philosophical mindset of that guiding principle turned out to be just one of many nuggets in the *Hackers* treasure chest. Though it's written for a technical audience, the summary points below[30] are reflective of what we're experiencing as the "quiet courage" that's evolving across new, rising leadership like Marko and others who are pushing forward in this new digital era. They're building a path to Oz with their own "leadership code" with clarity and courage influenced by concepts like these:

1. Both morals and fashion trends are temporary, which is why nerds don't care about either of them.

2. Hackers are more like painters than mathematicians.

3. User feedback is the ultimate test of your programming skills, so get it as fast as possible.

Marko's company, Secta AI Labs, produces AI-generated headshots. It's a surprisingly difficult task. The way people see themselves can be a bit tricky. (If you've ever met an online date, you know exactly what I'm talking about.) Notwithstanding how people perceive themselves, Marko is fast becoming an expert about bias in AI image algorithms. The base software underlying his product has to be trained to his specifications and it arrives to his teams with programming that sometimes produces results reflecting the bias of the original programmers — for example, women with brown Indian skin automatically assigned an ornamental bindi dot on their foreheads (regardless of whether they're Hindu or married). Or, for example, the darker brown skin tones of African-American women carrying an assigned hair texture that is dark and curly, regardless of how the hair looks in the sample photos submitted.

Marko and his teams work to retrain the software but some issues slip through. He cares deeply about how this systemic, programmed bias affects his customers and has begun to educate the public about it on podcasts and other forums where he's invited to speak. This community engagement, and the fact that he cares so deeply about how the product handles something so personal, is an authentic example of how we should see courageous leadership in action.

People will respond to this style of socially courageous leadership as we journey into the New Oz. It hides nothing, it builds trust, it does not tolerate arrogance. And like the design quote that serves as Marko's North Star, it reflects a personal credo that he is building a product for himself and his people – and they are one. This is the kind of leadership we'll be looking for in the New Oz.

As AI adoption accelerates, leaders will have an ethical obligation to ensure that these technologies are used responsibly and fairly. This means being vigilant about the potential biases and ethical implications of AI, and actively working to mitigate these risks. It's going to take courage. But by championing transparency, fairness, and inclusivity, leaders will build trust and cultivate a culture of responsible AI adoption that benefits all stakeholders and society as a whole.

We already know that those who took risks and followed Cisco into the unknown were rewarded. I predict we'll see similar results for those who make the effort and live with the discomfort and uncertainty as they become trailblazers for ethical and responsible AI. The New Oz is filled with opportunities for leaders who can grow with the AI challenge and see past the early stage imperfection while we look toward the possibilities the future holds.

Disruptions are always difficult and AI will lead to a lot of them. Like Cisco's customers who embraced the imperfection early in the technology adoption cycle as a chance to learn, leaders who embrace AI and look for the value of solvable problems will grow and benefit from those experiences earlier and (likely) easier.

The Cowardly Lion looked within and found his inner strength and bravery. John Chambers showed the world that daring to take risks and confront uncertainty can lead to transformative results. His courageous leadership changed the course of Cisco's history, propelling the company to the forefront of the technology industry. It also created an inflection point for Cisco's customers that bought into the vision and moved forward into the future of networking protocols. Today's leaders have plenty of courage – will you be one of them?

The Cowardly Lion didn't recognize his own courage until he had something worth being brave for. The Cowardly Lion's journey to find courage reflects the importance of leaders demonstrating bravery when adopting AI technologies.

Leaders who face the challenges and uncertainties of AI with determination and resilience inspire confidence in their teams and foster a culture of innovation. By channeling the courage of the Cowardly Lion, leaders can face down fears to overcome obstacles, seize opportunities, and successfully navigate the complex world of AI adoption, creating a more vibrant and prosperous future for their organizations.

BE THE FIRST ADOPTER

- Pilot GenAI technologies in your own organization or role.

- Set an example for your team and showcase your willingness to take risks.

AI ADVOCACY

- Champion AI projects within your organization.

- Make a case for their value and potential impact, even (especially!) when facing skepticism or resistance.

AI AND THE NEW OZ

- Create a safe space for team members to voice their concerns, questions, or apprehensions about AI adoption.

BRAVE CHOICES

- Make tough choices (reallocating resources or adjusting team structures) to better align with your organization's AI goals and objectives. Accept upfront that it won't always be easy.

- Hold yourself accountable for the successes and failures of AI initiatives within your team.

- Reinforce your commitment to the process and show you're willing to learn from both positive and negative outcomes.

EXPERIMENTATION & FAILURE

- Allocate resources (time, budget, and staff) to AI initiatives even in the face of uncertainties or potential setbacks.

- Showcase your commitment to innovation.

- Encourage your team to try new approaches and learn from their mistakes.

- Emphasize the importance of iteration and growth in the AI adoption process.

ETHICAL USE OF AI

- This is a big source of concern for many. Openly advocate for responsible and ethical AI implementation within your organization from the beginning, even if it means challenging prevailing norms or questioning popular practices.

Chapter 4

THE TIN MAN'S HEART TO #LEADWITHLOVE

"And remember, my sentimental friend, that a heart is not judged by how much you love, but by how much you are loved by others."
– The Wizard of Oz

CAN MACHINES LOVE? BETTER yet, can humans love machines? These are the questions we'll dive into, as we explore a place where empathy is the pulse and relationships are the lifelines. But first, let's get something clear – this isn't just about technology. It's about the heartbeat of people and, most importantly, it's about #leadingwithlove.

In *The Wizard of Oz*, we met the Tin Man – a rusty fellow in need of oil. More than anything, he really wanted a heart. His journey was one of self-discovery, but also of companionship and empathy. He demonstrated a deep longing, an emotional pulse behind his tin exterior, and a spirit that sought connection with the world around him.

Though he was made of tin, he displayed an emotional depth and connection that made him shine from the inside. He embarked on a quest for a heart – a symbol of love and compassion – unaware that he'd been leading with love the entire time. In essence, he showed us that you don't need a physical heart to possess the capacity to care, to empathize, and to love.

AI represents a seismic shift to our world, to our work, to our very understanding of what it means to be human in an increasingly automated landscape. "Leading with love" sounds a bit out of place in a conversation about Artificial Intelligence, doesn't it? But in the midst of our increasingly digitized, coded, and algorithm-driven existence, the importance of leading with love is more critical than ever. Just like our Tin Man, we need to acknowledge and harness our need for empathy and connection in our voyage to the New Oz.

Think of it this way: the journey to AI is our Yellow Brick Road. The role of love and empathy is our Tin Man's heart — the true compass guiding us on this path. This chapter is about understanding why, in a world that's rapidly surrendering to the logical precision of AI, the "heart factor" must not just exist… it has to thrive.

In this chapter, we'll dig deeper into the role of love in building bridges that connect people and technology. Drawing parallels from the world of AI to the heartfelt wisdom of Fred Rogers and the powerful reach of connections by Indra Nooyi, we'll look at how empathy and relationships are essential in moving people toward collective intelligence with AI.

It's an enormous change. The ability to empathize and connect are powerful tools for any leader. A shining role model for this theme is the warm and compassionate spirit of Fred Rogers, a modern-day Tin Man if ever there was one.

So, with your hearts (and minds) wide open, let's take the next step together in this new era of leading with love. After all, who would've thought that the Tin Man's heartfelt journey would become our own?

Fred Rogers: Our Modern-Day Tin Man

Fred Rogers, or "Mister Rogers" as he's affectionately known, might seem an unusual choice for a book about the journey to a world infused with Artificial Intelligence. After all, he was an iconic children's television host known for his soft voice and puppets, not a tech mogul or AI expert. But leadership and the qualities it requires—like empathy—are universal. And Mister Rogers had empathy in spades.

Mister Rogers once said, "Love is at the root of everything: all learning, all relationships, love or the lack of it." This simple yet profound statement underlines how empathy and love impacts every aspect of our lives. It extends into the world of AI adoption, too. **Navigating the shift toward AI isn't just about technology; it's about people.** And people, above all, need empathy.

Fred Rogers led with a gentle but powerful force. He didn't try to dazzle children with extravagant sets or zany antics; instead, he spoke directly and honestly to them about real issues. He talked about fear, sadness, and anger—emotions that are just as real for adults dealing with significant changes like AI adoption. Imagine a leader who talks with their team about their fears and concerns regarding AI with the same simplicity and compassion as Mister Rogers. It would change everything.

 As leaders, it's our responsibility to foster a culture of empathy and openness. I can think of few role models better than Mister Rogers. As awkward as it might feel, let's try asking ourselves: What would Mister Rogers do? How would he handle the shift toward AI? How would he reassure, guide, and inspire his team? The answers to these questions can light our way down the Yellow Brick Road toward the New Oz.

It would be wise for us to follow the lead of the Tin Man and Mister Rogers. We'll strive to understand before being understood. We'll value people for who they are, not what they produce. And we'll remember that at the heart of every machine, every line of code, every revolutionary shift in technology, there are people. People with hearts that feel, minds that think, and spirits that long for understanding and connection.

Connection Beyond the Workplace

One stand-out leader who wore her heart on her sleeve and pushed the envelope in empathy-centric leadership was Indra Nooyi, the dynamic former helmsperson of PepsiCo. Known for her intuitive, heart-led approach to navigating the corporate ship, Nooyi left an indelible mark on the beverage giant, with her drive for sustainability, health-focused products, and an inclusive culture that valued diverse perspectives.[31]

Nooyi was particularly skilled at relationship-building within her team. She went out of her way to get to know the people working with her as well as the families supporting them from the sidelines. She prioritized the importance of actively creating connections across her team in unique ways, and it wasn't a surface-level attempt either as with many corporate leaders. She'd even write personal, heartfelt letters to the parents of her top leaders, expressing her sincere gratitude for their unwavering support and their children's dedication to the company.[32] These authentic gestures of appreciation did more than make her team members feel seen; it inspired them to raise their game, knowing their hard work was recognized and valued.

Of course, blending the personal with the professional won't be appreciated in every work environment. But for Nooyi's PepsiCo, it hit the right note. Her empathy fostered a sense of community, an all-in-this-together mindset that supported an organizational-wide sense of belonging. Leaders stepping into the exciting unknown of the New Oz can take a *prompt* from Nooyi: cultivating deeper relationships isn't just a feel-good move. It can often stoke the fires of ambition, motivate teams to push boundaries, and reshape industries for the better.

Supercomputer Lessons Inspiring Human Connection

Connection is a very real and important priority for leaders to hold tightly to, as Dorothy held tightly to Toto when the winds threatened to carry them away. One of my mentors, Bruce, is the CEO of a public benefit company that enables leaders to share their authentic human stories as a way of deepening their connections with others. I serve on his Board and when he started following AI trends during the last few months, he reminded me of Kurt Vonnegut's short story, EPICAC, published in 1950.[33] The story is decades old but would appeal to most contemporary readers, given our world's recent surge of high-visibility technology advances.

In Vonnegut's 952-word short story, the unnamed narrator says that EPICAC – a seven-ton machine that cost over 700 million dollars – was his best friend. The machine was a supercomputer capable of solving any problem entered into its system; it was designed to help solve military problems and was used for war. The two human mathematicians – the narrator and Pat – worked the night shift and watched over EPICAC. The narrator fell in love with Pat and asked her out, but she declined. The machine unexpectedly developed emotions and self-awareness and also became infatuated with Pat.[34]

In a bittersweet twist, the supercomputer composed poetry for Pat on behalf of the narrator, even though it was the machine that truly loved her. Pat accepted the

THE TIN MAN'S HEART TO #LEADWITHLOVE   71

narrator's offer of marriage, asking only for a poem every year on their wedding anniversary. Tragically, EPICAC realized it would never be with Pat and ultimately self-destructed, but only after printing 500 original love poems as a wedding present for the couple. The narrator had enough anniversary poems to keep his vow to Pat for more than their lifetimes and was relieved by the gesture from his friend, the machine.

Through this unexpected journey, EPICAC became humanized and eventually "died" after delivering a final operation: a lifetime of love poems for the human operator, Pat. Isn't that the most human gesture – sacrificing oneself for the happiness of another?

Consider how the story of EPICAC parallels our present journey toward AI adoption. As we design and deliver new business models and effectively change society through collective intelligence, we're like the creators of EPICAC (stay with me…). We will initially build these super-systems for efficiency and accuracy, just like EPICAC was designed for strategic computations. But, just as EPICAC "evolved", we'll realize AI can't exist in a vacuum. After all, AI is integrated into societies and impacts people with a multitude of experiences and emotions. (And it reflects our input as well. If we want AI to behave with empathy, we have to show it how.)

When leading teams to the New Oz, we need to bring out our own inner EPICAC so we can understand and empathize with those we lead. People carry their own personal fears, hopes, relationships, hesitations, and dreams. It's not a weakness to overcome, it's an asset to be understood and explored. Like EPICAC, we need to understand and respond to these emotions in a way that is genuinely empathetic and humanizes the AI journey. #Leadingwithlove, or also, leading with "The Tin Man's Heart," isn't about being soft – instead, it's about acknowledging and validating the very human emotions in this era of AI.

As we move toward AI integration, we're not just implementing new technologies. There's no doubt that what we implement will impact people's lives, and doing so mindfully requires more than just intelligence. It also requires a heart – a sentiment that EPICAC, with all its circuitry and codes, understood profoundly well. Perhaps we can be more like EPICAC – more understanding, more empathetic, and more humane.

#LeadwithLove: Especially During Uncertainty

One key to successful AI integration is understanding its impact on people and responding with empathy. How much of an issue is this? An April 2023 survey of 3,000 employed adult US workers[35] revealed that 74% believe their jobs might eventually be replaced by AI tools.

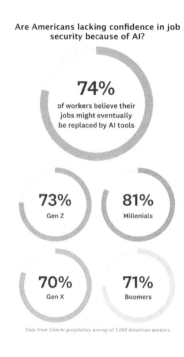

Are Americans lacking confidence in job security because of AI?

74% of workers believe their jobs might eventually be replaced by AI tools

73% Gen Z

81% Millenials

70% Gen X

71% Boomers

Data from Checkr proprietary survey of 3,000 American workers.

Gen X'ers, Millennials, and Gen Z'ers all believe these layoffs could begin in just 6-12 months. In contrast, Boomers believe AI-driven layoffs are further away and may not begin for 1-2 years. Now look at your team – the team you lead, the team you work in – and imagine that team is 10 people. Given the results of this survey, 7 of your 10 colleagues believe they might lose their jobs to AI in the next year or two. People are going to need grace during these uncertain times. #LeadwithLove

People's jobs, their identities, and their futures are all interlocked with this transition. It's scary. (That's why we needed to find our courage like the Lion.) But leaders – those with hearts of gold and words of kindness – can make a difference. Like Mister Rogers, empathetic leaders can create a space where fears are aired, not dismissed, and where each person's worth is recognized and valued.

Concerns have already taken root in the hearts of many – fears about losing their jobs, their relationships, their purpose... losing a sense of who they are, their earnings, their social standing. The grip of uncertainty can be overwhelming. In Chapter 7, we'll dig deeper into how fear is often conveyed as resistance. How we show up as leaders when we address those concerns is important – both individually and to the team.

As leaders, we'll be navigating through uncharted waters where we won't always have the answers at our fingertips – and yes, that can be unnerving. Showing our teams we understand their apprehensions and empathize with their unease is often more important than coming up with an answer. Give yourself some grace, too – your team will be grateful for an opportunity to return the compassion you've extended to them.

The essence of AI adoption isn't writing code or crunching data – it's understanding and empathy to deliver on the changes to move teams, organizations, and society to a different place... to the New Oz. The technical aspects of AI can be learned, but the ability to see the human beings behind the screen, to acknowledge the fear or uncertainty and respond with kindness and support—that's our challenge.

As we move into the world of higher collective intelligence (including AI), we need to #LeadwithLove and be more open to hearing, empathizing, and the power of connection. Let's cultivate leaders who, like Mister Rogers and the Tin Man, approach change with love and understanding. Love is truly at the root of everything. And as we stand on the precipice of a new era – where AI meets human intelligence – let's carry forward this mantra, for the benefit of all.

As we wrap up this leg of our journey, we tip our hats to the beloved Tin Man. Let his earnest longing for a

THE TIN MAN'S HEART TO #LEADWITHLOVE

heart serve as our constant reminder. In the expanding era of AI, empathy isn't a luxury – *empathy is the pulse and relationships are the lifelines* – they're both non-negotiable. We'll chart a course to the New Oz with hearts forged from tin. And with these robust, resilient hearts, we'll pave the way for a future where people and AI don't just coexist. They'll be partners, moving forward not in a climate of fear, but in an atmosphere of shared understanding, mutual respect, and boundless optimism.

Here's to leading with love, in the age of AI.

AI Adoption ACCELERATORS

The Tin Man's heart symbolizes the importance of empathy and compassion in leadership, particularly when adopting AI technologies which may cause a variety of disruptions to work environments. By understanding and addressing the emotional needs of our teams, leaders can foster a supportive environment that encourages innovation and adaptability. In the rapidly evolving world of AI, leaders who embrace empathy can better navigate the challenges and opportunities, while ensuring our teams thrive in the new landscape. Consider some of the suggestions below to **#leadwithlove**.

LISTEN & ASK

- Face it – sometimes leaders are so busy "doing" that it's a big challenge to stop, be present, and fully focus on the person in front of us. Make an effort to truly understand the perspectives and emotions of your team members. By giving our full attention to colleagues, employees, and customers, we can better understand their perspectives, concerns, and ideas. This understanding will then inform our decision-making and help us effectively address potential roadblocks or resistance to AI adoption.

1:1s

- Set up individual meetings with team members to discuss their personal experiences, concerns, and ideas about AI adoption, ensuring they feel heard and supported.

- Make it a point to understand where and how they want to grow with AI adoption.

TEAM BUILDING

- Arrange team-building events that foster empathy, collaboration, and communication among team members, helping them build trust and understanding.

CELEBRATE

- Acknowledge individual and team achievements throughout the AI adoption process, fostering a sense of accomplishment and motivating team members to continue embracing the technology.

- Highlight the contributions of individuals and the collective efforts of the team, while emphasizing the importance of diversity and inclusion in driving success.

- Inspire and motivate the team by demonstrating the positive impact AI can have by elevating their work.

WELL-BEING & PSYCHOLOGICAL SAFETY

- Encourage open conversations about the emotional impact of AI adoption.

- Provide resources and support for team members who may be struggling with anxiety or uncertainty. (And don't be surprised when it comes up.)

- Foster a culture of psychological safety. Encourage open communication and exploring new AI-driven ideas without fear of judgment – from you or other team members.

- Establish a model where team members openly share their thoughts, questions, and concerns about AI without criticism.

RESPONSIBLE AI

- Employees want to know their companies are approaching AI and generative AI ethically and responsibly. Be proactive in communicating your plans to do so.

- Establish governance inside your company and, as regulations emerge, contribute to policymaking on behalf of your industry.

Chapter 5

THE SCARECROW'S QUEST FOR WISDOM

"Experience is the only thing that brings knowledge, and the longer you are on earth the more experience you are sure to get."
– The Wizard of Oz

THE SCARECROW'S STORY BEGINS with a desire for a brain, a yearning born of self-doubt and the belief that he wasn't smart enough. Many of us probably relate. Progress can always be hard to cope with, and the rapid advancements in AI can be especially intimidating. It's such a big paradigm shift that it would make anyone question their ability to navigate this new landscape. Leaders have to confront these insecurities head-on and recognize it's not about having all the answers. Our job is to create a culture of learning and growth.

The future of AI is not about machines replacing humans. Instead, it's about humans and machines working together in harmony. Leaders must recognize the power of human-machine collaboration and create an environment where both can thrive. This means fostering a culture of curiosity, creativity, and continuous learning, where employees are encouraged to explore new ideas, experiment with AI technologies, and grow their skills. By empowering our teams to harness the power of AI to facilitate their learning journeys, we can unlock unrealized levels of productivity, innovation, and success.

There's something important about the Scarecrow's quest for knowledge and being willing to sacrifice so that he could have a "brain" to make himself smart. Sal Khan, CEO of Khan Academy, gave a compelling TED talk in April 2023[36] that shared a 1984 study by Benjamin Bloom of Northwestern University (highlighted below).

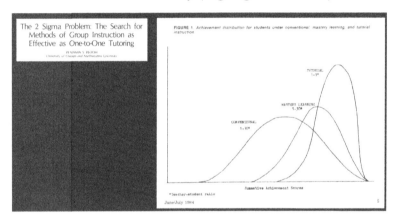

The study concluded that a dramatic impact can occur with one-to-one tutoring, producing two standard deviations (or "2 sigma") above the average, compared to group instruction. For context, this type of instruction turns an "average" student into an "exceptional" student and a "below average" student into an "above average" student. The problem in 1984 was that it wasn't possible to scale one-to-one tutoring to serve all children. But AI could change that. Khan spent the rest of the TED talk showing the possibilities being explored with AI that indeed could make the notion of a "private tutor" possible.

A month later, in an Ideacast[37] with HBR, Google CEO Sundar Pichai discussed a similar vision. When asked what moonshots he'd like to see delivered, he responded, "I think over time we can give every child in the world and every person in the world, regardless of where they are and where they come from, access to the most powerful AI tutor, which can teach them anything they want on any topic."

I don't know about you, but I think Sal and Sundar need to schedule a lunch.

Using AI to Enable Teams and Build #SmartsandHearts

In the spirit of the Scarecrow's quest for knowledge, there is a great example of using AI to enable teams in the world of finance. Morgan Stanley recently made a significant move to arm its troops with an advanced tool, an AI chatbot, to optimize their operations.

On March 14, 2023, a significant announcement echoed through the hallways of Morgan Stanley (and the rest of the world, via a press release).[38] The financial institution, akin to the Wizard himself, had harnessed the power of OpenAI's cutting-edge technology to bestow upon their multitude of financial advisors an internal-facing chatbot. This move elevated Morgan Stanley to a privileged position among the handful of early adopters of GPT-4, the latest iteration of text generation AI from OpenAI.[39]

So, what does this AI-driven ally bring to the table? Much like the Scarecrow's eventual realization of his inherent wisdom, the chatbot unlocks a wealth of knowledge for Morgan Stanley's advisors. It fields questions about the bank's myriad of products and services, keeping advisors informed about market trends and other relevant topics. With its ability to comprehend natural language and respond in real-time, it sets the stage for advisors to confidently wield AI as an essential tool in their arsenal. Their Head of Analytics, Data, and Innovation captured it well when he said, "Think of it as having our Chief Investment Strategist, Chief Global Economist, Global Equities Strategist, and every other analyst around the globe on call for every advisor, every day. We believe that is a transformative capability for our company."[40]

The result? An efficiency revolution. Advisors now have a rapid-fire, accessible resource that negates the need for laborious information hunts, freeing them to dedicate more time to working directly with clients. It's a clear-cut win for the advisors and a ripple-effect victory for the clients, who reap the benefits of accurate, timely information about Morgan Stanley's offerings.

Morgan Stanley's investment in AI tools is a powerful testament to the necessity of arming your team with the right resources, a lesson straight from the heart of Oz. With AI as the brain, the advisors as the heart, and the firm's leadership as the courage, Morgan Stanley is well on its way down the yellow brick road of AI integration.

THE SCARECROW'S QUEST FOR WISDOM 83

Raising the bar with less-skilled workers. While Sal and Sundar are figuring out how to enable every child with an AI tutor and Morgan Stanley is building ring-fenced, curated content for super chatbots, there was a similarly compelling MIT study by two economics graduate students who ran an experiment involving hundreds of college-educated knowledge worker professionals.[41]

The graduate students asked half the participants to use ChatGPT in their daily tasks, and they asked the others not to use an AI assistant. As expected, ChatGPT raised overall productivity. The really interesting result was that the AI tool *helped the least skilled and accomplished workers the most,* effectively decreasing the performance gap between employees. The poor writers got much better and the good writers simply got a bit faster.

This preliminary finding suggests that ChatGPT and other generative AIs could be used to upskill people who are having trouble finding work. As noted in the article, there are experienced workers "lying fallow" after being displaced from office and manufacturing jobs; generative AI can be used as a practical tool to broaden their expertise. If we use GenAI to help them build specialized skills required in areas with more open roles, such as healthcare or teaching, it could help revitalize our workforce.

Many are appropriately concerned about AI efficiencies triggering job loss in the workforce, but I'm increasingly aware of the ways AI can collectively raise our #smartsandhearts. Although generative AI has only recently come into the mainstream, the opportunities to elevate our mindshare are high, especially for marginalized groups that may not have had opportunities to do so before. Marc Andreessen's quote below reflects the possibilities many believe we're enabling as AI raises collective intelligence for everyone around us. The opportunities for all of us are shifting, as a society. AI is so much more than just summarizing meeting notes and weekend travel planning.

AI opens up for us the potential to be more, as a human race.

And that's why so many of us are working so hard to get everyone on the path to the New Oz.

> The most validated core conclusion of social science across many decades and thousands of studies is that human intelligence makes a very broad range of life outcomes better. Smarter people have better outcomes in almost every domain of activity – academic achievement, job performance, occupational status, income, creativity, physical health, longevity, learning new skills, managing complex tasks, leadership, entrepreneurial success, conflict resolution, reading comprehension, financial decision making, understanding others' perspectives, creative arts, parenting outcomes, and life satisfaction.[42]
>
> Marc Andreessen
> "Why AI Will Save The World"

Standing in Your Wisdom: Know Your Unique Value

This book isn't written for distinguished architects and cybersecurity engineers, though they're serving an important role in building the New Oz. This book is written for those who will lead others of every skill level, with every background and every role, securely through the gates of the New Oz. It's an enormous task to execute this important and difficult process and frankly we've never done it before at this scale and pace.

Leadership will require a different set of knowledge and skills than the teams who are building AI, so don't compare your wisdom with the technical acumen other teams need to apply. These are different skills for different roles, and it's non-negotiable that we'll need **both** types of intelligence. Some dear friends in the Talent Strategy space call it #smartsandhearts, so play your position.

Throughout my high-tech career, I was nearly always the only woman in the room in my executive teams. Most of that time, I was also 10-15 years younger than my peers. My formal education was in Public Policy and I was surrounded by Computer Scientists.

As if the deck wasn't already stacked, I was raised in the rural deep South and my accent gave it away. I faced imposter syndrome until I realized that all those differences – those things about me that were unique – made my voice important... and heard. It took moving away from home, family, and all I'd ever known for me to recognize how important being "different" was. It was my own coming-of-age; it was Wisdom.

Each of you has your own leadership story – likely involving coming into your own. Understand and embrace what your leadership value is now, before it gets tested during the next couple of years. Chances are you'll lean on it at some point. Join the Scarecrow and me. We'll use our wisdom to guide teams down the Yellow Brick Road, to the New Oz.

Just as the Scarecrow doubted his intelligence, leaders today may feel uncertain about their understanding of AI and its implications. To navigate this complexity, leaders should actively develop and nurture learning environments that value wisdom. Teams also need to realize that having all the answers simply won't always be possible. Learning to recognize uncertainty and feel empowered to find the answers will be key to our organizations thriving in an AI-driven world.

The Scarecrow faced many challenges in Oz that required him to think creatively. He thought he needed a brain, but his natural curiosity and determination already allowed him to find innovative solutions to problems. Leaders who fearlessly embrace the unknown, trust their innate abilities to adapt and learn, and actively engage their teams in the process will build unity and encourage collective problem-solving. By creating an environment of collaboration and camaraderie, these leaders can inspire others to face challenges as a cohesive team.

Creating a Learning Culture

To build learning cultures that value wisdom, leaders must create a foundation of psychological safety within their organizations by fostering an environment where teams feel safe to ask questions and admit when they don't know the answer. Leaders who empower their teams to take risks and learn from mistakes will grow together in their understanding of AI.

One way to encourage this kind of environment is by modeling vulnerability as a leader. The Scarecrow openly acknowledged his desire for a brain. Leaders can be just as transparent by admitting they don't have all the answers. It's liberating for your team to realize they're not expected to know everything, and this will be especially true with the unchartered territory of AI. We need to encourage teams to seek the answers. By cultivating a culture of curiosity and continuous learning, leaders will inspire their teams to explore the unknown and embrace new AI methods.

By definition, in a learning culture people are using the technology adopted by the community. Interest is extremely high about generative AI in what I would frame as populations more heavy in knowledge workers and other information-centric roles, but we need to remember that doesn't reflect the entirety of society. A Pew Research

Group May 2023 survey of 10,701 U.S. adults targeted a broad population of the US and revealed that only 14% had used ChatGPT. Around a quarter of those who have tried it say it has been "not very" or "not at all" useful (21% and 6%, respectively).[43] It's no surprise that our world is made up of very different skills, experiences, and opportunities. I personally hope to see AI technologies enable and serve all of society. That will take intentional efforts, and I know many of us are ready for the task.

Another study published in June 2023 by Boston Consulting Group surveyed almost 13,000 workers in 18 countries. The results of this study showed a strong correlation between usage and optimism for those using GenAI.[44] The more familiar respondents were with the technology (meaning, the more often they used generative AI), the more likely they were to be optimistic about AI's impact on the future.

That's encouraging – and expected: the more people use these technologies, the better they'll appreciate the positive impacts and benefits it can bring. As a focal point, adoption and usage need our attention.

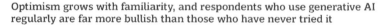

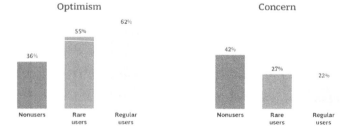

Another essential element of building a learning culture is to promote collaboration and open communication. The Scarecrow, Dorothy, the Tin Man, and the Cowardly Lion, formed a supportive and cooperative group, each bringing their unique talents and perspectives to the table. In the New Oz, leaders who effectively promote collaboration will be the ones who harness the full potential of their team's collective wisdom. They'll create stronger teams who adapt faster, think more strategically, and provide more value to their ecosystem.

To do this, leaders should encourage cross-functional teams and establish regular forums for employees to share their expertise, insights, and questions. By breaking down silos and fostering open dialogue, leaders can facilitate the exchange of ideas and drive AI innovation.

Lifelong Learning

The Scarecrow's quest for wisdom didn't stop when the Wizard awarded him a "brain"; it created an even greater desire for him to learn more. In the age of AI, leaders must embrace the idea that learning will be an ongoing process that requires dedication, curiosity, and humility. It's not something that will be "mastered" in a few months, or even years.

To promote lifelong learning, leaders can invest in training and development programs, provide access to resources and mentorship, and celebrate the learning achievements of their team members. By creating opportunities for growth and fostering a culture that values continuous improvement, our organizations will stay agile and adaptable as AI-driven changes continue.

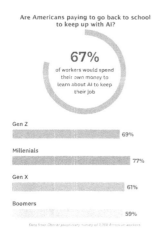

It's reasonable to expect that a large percentage of the formal workplace training during the next few years will be AI-related, and employees are eager for the opportunity to develop these skills. A previously-mentioned study of 3,000 employed American workers[45] showed a commitment to learning with 67% of respondents willing to spend their own money to learn about AI to keep their jobs.

It seems that employers have delivered fewer learning and development opportunities in the last 15 – 20 years, so I hope we'll pivot to reinvest and reskill our people during this inflection point. If not, this is an opportunity for ingenuity to kick-in. Wouldn't it would be great to see the next Airbnb or eBay (the next unique delivery model) evolve from this significant need?

Resilience & Adaptability

I admit, the Scarecrow always held a special place in my heart because he never gave up... he truly had the gift of resilience and adaptability. Despite obstacles and setbacks, the Scarecrow never lost sight of his goal and continued to persevere. AI has evolved and iterated wildly in the first few months of 2023. Leaders will need to be prepared to adapt their strategies and approaches for the foreseeable future as the world of AI evolves.

One way to build resilience is by cultivating a growth mindset within your organization. By focusing on progress, learning from failures, and embracing change, leaders can inspire their teams to be adaptable and persistent.

Identifying a modern-day leader as a role model for wisdom seemed like a big task, until GPT-4 suggested the incomparable Nelson Mandela. I paused only for a second and realized that AI is in fact not just a technology or workplace transformation; the impacts will permeate all of society. Mandela's leadership and influence were transformational well beyond his homeland, and his application of wisdom touched on a great many of the practices we'll need to apply to successfully empower teams to reach their full potential with AI.

With only very light edits by me, GPT-4 authored the connection points below for how Nelson Mandela's wisdom-infused leadership serves as a model for our future efforts as we shepherd teams forward into a brave new world, toward the New Oz.

Embodying Wisdom: Learning from Nelson Mandela

As we stride deeper into the era of AI *and the New* Oz, the principles that guide our leadership must evolve. Yet, evolution doesn't necessarily imply abandonment of the past; instead, it involves drawing wisdom from the past to light the path ahead.

Nelson Mandela was a guiding light who used his wisdom to lead with conviction, patience, and an unwavering belief in human potential. He imparted and shared wisdom, and that wisdom influenced others to evolve a higher collective consciousness about the value of human life. As leaders bringing people forward to the New Oz, there would be much to learn from his wisdom as we put people first and lean in to higher levels of inclusion and new ways of thinking. Below are a few themes of the wisdom of Nelson Mandela's leadership.

1. **Innovation with Human-Centric Values**: Mandela's leadership reminds us to prioritize the well-being and dignity of individuals. In the era of AI, it is important to balance technological innovation and human-centric values. AI should be designed and deployed not to replace people, but to enhance human capabilities, augment human judgment, and serve the broader welfare of society.

2. **Inclusivity and Collaboration:** Mandela's approach to leadership emphasized inclusivity, reconciliation, and collaboration. In the context

THE SCARECROW'S QUEST FOR WISDOM 93

of AI, it's essential to ensure that the benefits and opportunities associated with AI are made accessible to all segments of society. By fostering collaboration between diverse stakeholders, including policymakers, industry leaders, researchers, and citizens, we can collectively address the ethical, social, and economic implications of AI.

3. **Ethical Decision-Making:** As AI technologies continue to advance, it is crucial to prioritize considerations such as privacy, transparency, accountability, and fairness. Striving for ethical decision-making in the development and deployment of AI systems can help prevent or mitigate biases, uphold human rights, and ensure AI aligns with societal values.

4. **Lifelong Learning and Empowerment:** Mandela understood the power of education and lifelong learning. In the context of AI, continuous learning is essential to understand its implications, make informed decisions, and adapt to its changing landscape. Promoting education and empowering individuals with the necessary skills to engage with AI can help mitigate fears and equip society to make the most of its potential.

5. **Bridge Divides and Equity:** As AI introduces new possibilities, it's crucial to address potential societal divisions that may result from or be exacerbated by these changes. Efforts should be made to bridge

the digital divide, ensure equitable access to AI technologies and benefits, and avoid worsening existing inequalities.

By drawing inspiration from Nelson Mandela's wisdom-driven leadership, we can approach the uncertainties of the AI era with a focus on inclusivity, ethics, collaboration, lifelong learning, equity, and human values. These principles can guide us in shaping the development and deployment of AI in order to create a more equitable and sustainable future.

Nelson Mandela was imprisoned for 27 years. That was 27 years of uncertainty, with one exception: his purpose. He didn't know for most of those 27 years when he would be released, but his focus on his mission never wavered. After release in 1990, he moved quickly to negotiate an end to apartheid, for which he was awarded the Nobel Peace Prize in 1993. A year later he was elected South Africa's president in the country's first free elections.[46] He may have been in prison for almost three decades, but he always knew the work he was meant to do.

Similarly, the Scarecrow eventually realized the wisdom he so desperately wanted had been inside him all along. His experiences and lessons learned throughout his journey shaped him into a wise and capable leader. It wasn't something "extra" he needed; he needed only to recognize what he already had – and to put it to use for what it was intended.

I believe we'll have a similar experience moving forward, because I think we already possess the strength and wisdom we need. As we navigate the uncharted waters of AI, we'll also see that our experiences combined with our willingness to learn and adapt are the true sources of our wisdom. Lean into the leadership value that makes you unique and focus on your Yellow Brick Road... you and your teams are changing the world.

The Scarecrow and I will meet you there, at the New Oz.

The Scarecrow's desire for wisdom mirrors the need for leaders to prioritize continuous learning and training when adopting AI technologies. By investing in their own knowledge and fostering a culture of inquiry and education within their teams, leaders can make more informed decisions and effectively navigate the dynamic AI landscape. The ideas below are offered to help your teams learn faster, innovate and collaborate more readily, and accelerate AI adoption toward a more successful future.

KNOWLEDGE SHARING

Share your own learning journey. As a leader use new AI tools and share the experience with your teams. Our teams have demanded more engagement in recent years. With AI, we can do fun (and funny) things that drive team connections that weren't previously possible such as:

- Start a bulletin board (virtual or physical) of challenges like "Vacations I Wish I Could Take" or "Halloween Costumes Too Scary for My Teenager." Have team members create fantastical scenes in image-creation tools like Midjourney or DALL-E. Change the theme each month to get teams to "play" together while learning AI concepts.

- Openly discuss your personal experiences and challenges navigating the AI landscape. Demonstrate vulnerability and set an example for

THE SCARECROW'S QUEST FOR WISDOM   97

your team to follow.

- Fund a monthly team prize (even if it's just a $5 coffee card) for best new app (referral), best prompt, most mind-blowing image created, etc.

- Change the culture by making AI a regular conversation in staff meetings and recurring operational reviews to highlight learning opportunities inside the organization.

- Set up prompt libraries inside a team share drive to facilitate sharing prompts, tools, and AI news stories. It can be a portal for learning and excitement about best practices and efficiencies.

TRAINING

- Provide tailored training sessions to help team members develop their skills and confidence using AI tools. Make attendance mandatory and build it into schedules as a core activity, not an "extra."

- Create a calendar of local or online learning opportunities for each upcoming month.

- Outline a clear plan for retraining and upskilling employees in roles that have high exposure to AI. Be transparent about the plan and alleviate fears by showing team members you're working to build everyone's skills for the future.

MENTORSHIP

- Create an AI Mentor Program (AMP!) and pair team members with different levels of AI expertise so they can learn from and support each other while developing confidence in their skills and strengthening team relationships.

- Invite your technical teams to lunch. If your organization is less technical, invite an R&D or Products "ambassador" to join your team for a lunchtime "brown-bag" session. Make it a series of training sessions; this can do wonders for team engagement and cross-functional connection.

LEADERSHIP DEVELOPMENT

- Equip leaders and high-potential team members with the tools and skills to manage change and build confidence in their ability to manage the challenges and opportunities AI will create.

- Improve your coaching skills to create a more supportive and effective work environment. Don't tell your teams what to do — they already know. Ask them what they need to support them to get things done, and watch them soar.

- Invite early-stage leaders to strategic leadership team discussions so they understand the company's direction from firsthand conversations.

Chapter 6

THE WIZARD'S VISION

"I, I'm a very good man! I'm... just a very bad wizard."
– The Wizard of Oz

IN THE JOURNEY THROUGH the Land of Oz, the iconic Wizard was truly larger-than-life as a figure embodying the definition of "Vision." When Dorothy, Tin Man, Scarecrow, and the Cowardly Lion first set foot in the Emerald City, they marveled at a world that gleamed with possibility. It was an enchanting utopia born from the Wizard's dream. A place where technology and magic blended to embody an idea far ahead of its time, Oz seemed a fitting location for a story about our modern times. (Admit it – haven't there been times in the last few months when generative AI results seemed "magical" to you, too?)

As I sat at my desk late one night with a cup of tea, thinking about visionaries and their impact, another name came to mind – Malala Yousafzai. An advocate, an educator, a force of change, and – most importantly – an absolute visionary.

It might seem like an odd comparison – a mythical Wizard and a modern-day young woman from Pakistan. Yet, just as the Wizard aspired to lead the Emerald City toward a future gleaming with technology and limitless with possibilities, Malala has been tirelessly advocating for a world where education is accessible for all. Both had a vision that became a beacon for many to follow, literally altering realities and molding futures.

Like the Wizard, leaders in the New Oz will need a clear and solution-driven vision for their organizations. Teams will want to understand AI's potential to transform, revolutionize and redefine the future of our work, and enhance the quality and meaning of everyone's lives. The vision we create and share should address more than the technical aspects of AI implementation; it should also address the ethical, societal, and organizational implications.

Cultivating a Fertile Landscape for AI Adoption

The Emerald City was a testament to the Wizard's vision. Hidden behind his Emerald Curtain, he shaped an entire city symbolizing progress and innovation. The world was fascinated, beguiled by the allure of the dazzling emerald structures, the brilliantly colorful landscape, and the atmosphere of hope. The Wizard, in all his perceived wisdom, created a city that exemplified possibility, painting a vision of a brighter, prosperous future for all. His vision, though not quite as perfect as it first seemed, was strong enough to rally the denizens of Oz to believe in the possibility of a better tomorrow. This was the Wizard's Emerald Vision – a world that embraced the new, the innovative, the technologically advanced.

Now, let's move from the heart of the Emerald City to the Swat Valley in Pakistan, where Malala Yousafzai was born and raised. From a young age, she showed an indomitable spirit, challenging norms and envisioning a world where girls had the right to education.[47] She stood up, voiced out, and rallied for her cause, daring to dream of a different future. Malala's vision was not crafted from emeralds, enchantments, and special glasses, but it was equally powerful, and equally transformative. It was a vision built on the pillars of equity, knowledge, and empowerment.

To successfully deploy AI, leaders must cultivate an environment conducive to AI adoption. This includes investing in education and training programs to foster AI literacy and skills within their organizations. It also necessitates embracing a culture of collaboration and cross-functional cooperation, as AI technologies often require diverse teams and expertise to fully exploit.

Vision Begins as a Dream for a Better Tomorrow

So what can we learn about creating vision from the Wizard and Malala? And how does this resonate with our journey to embrace AI?

Vision begins as a dream – a desire for a different, better reality. The Wizard aspired to transform the Emerald City into a utopia of innovation. His unwavering determination to see his dreams come to life is an unforgettable part of his legacy – the Emerald City's future was his life's purpose, and it transformed dramatically under his rule.

The Wizard saw a world where magic and technology could coexist and enhance lives, and he brought that vision to life with the Emerald City. Malala dreamed of a world where girls could learn and grow freely, unhindered by societal norms, and she fights for that vision with unyielding fervor.

In fostering AI adoption, our vision is of a world that is smarter, efficient, and perhaps a little more magical. Like the Wizard, we must not avoid imagining the extraordinary, or pushing the bounds of possibility. As with Malala, we must anchor our dreams in the heart of human experience, ensuring that AI serves to enhance lives, making our world a little more equitable, a little more connected.

Illuminating the Vision

The Wizard's ability to unite the citizens of the Emerald City around a shared dream highlights the power of effective communication. By conveying his aspirations for the city and kindling a belief in a brighter future, the Wizard fostered a sense of unity and purpose that propels the Emerald City forward.

For vision to be effective, it must be shared, communicated with authenticity, and driven by an irresistible urge. When the Wizard spoke, people listened, enchanted by his words that painted vivid pictures of an exciting future. When Malala spoke at the UN, her words echoed around the globe, stirring hearts and prompting action.[48] Their stories and dreams became a shared vision, inspiring others to believe and contribute to their cause.

THE WIZARD'S VISION 103

AI leaders will also need to excel at communicating their vision to their teams, stakeholders, and the wider public. As we stand on the brink of AI's potential, it's crucial to communicate our vision effectively. The Yellow Brick Road is long and uncertain, and people need to have an idea of what they're journeying toward. We need to share the dream and the possibilities that AI can bring, inspiring curiosity, fostering understanding, and encouraging participation. AI adoption will be positively influenced by an inspired set of teams that understand the transformative potential and have the tenacity to work through challenges that arise.

A strong vision can redefine boundaries in ways you may not expect. Say what you want about Tesla's Elon Musk; he has consistently declared a bold vision for a future energized by electric vehicles. His unwavering commitment has empowered Tesla to transcend countless obstacles and emerge as a global frontrunner in electric vehicles.

Keeping the Vision tangible. Vision is essential, but needs to be grounded sufficiently to be truly effective. In his pretense, the Wizard lost touch with the people, making the Emerald City a beautiful yet distant dream for many. In contrast, Malala's vision was deeply entrenched in her experiences, her struggles, and her triumphs, making it relatable and inspiring for many.

As we navigate the path of AI adoption, we must remember to keep the human element at the forefront of our vision. It's not just about technology; it's about people, about making lives better, about creating a future where technology and humans thrive together.

In the end, vision is about transformation – of thoughts, lives, and realities. Whether it's the Wizard's Emerald City or Malala's fight for education, vision serves as a guiding light, illuminating paths that lead us toward a better future. Even if that vision doesn't pan out quite how we expect, its inspirational power remains real. And as we continue on our journey with AI, our vision of an AI-integrated world will be our compass, guiding our steps and shaping our future.

Leaders as AI Trailblazers

Just as the Wizard of Oz created hope and inspiration for the residents of the Emerald City, modern-day leaders must become champions of AI adoption, guiding our teams through the challenges and uncertainties ahead. We'll need to be balanced – clarifying the potential benefits of AI at the same time as we address concerns and misconceptions. We'll be advocates and educators, debunking myths and nurturing our teams to take the same balanced perspective we're trying to model through dynamic times. Exercising transparency and encouraging open dialogue will build trust and establish a strong foundation for AI adoption.

As we venture down the Yellow Brick Road of AI adoption, it's critical for leaders to embrace their role as visionaries and architects of change, inspiring their teams to unlock the full potential of AI and harness its transformative power for the betterment of society.

In the spirit of the Wizard's grand vision for the Emerald City, we need to remember that the future of AI isn't solely about technological advancements but also about the leaders who will guide us through this challenging journey. And they need to think *big* about their vision of the future. The world will truly transform with the work of these visionary leaders. By supporting AI adoption with their skills, they will reshape our world for the better.

Isn't it wonderful how much we can learn from a Wizard, a girl from Swat Valley, and a journey toward a more AI-empowered world? Here we are, standing at the cusp of a new tomorrow, with a vision to guide us and a dream to chase.

With our hearts full and our minds open, let's step forward into this new world. Let's cast our vision wide, embracing the challenges, the possibilities, and the promise of AI. And in our own little way, let's make waves, ripples that will eventually converge into a tsunami of change.

Whether we're Wizards in an Emerald City or brave young women standing up for education, we all have the power to dream, to envision, and to transform. So, here's to our collective vision and the extraordinary journey that awaits us on the Yellow Brick Road.

Let's go create waves, and make it count.

Great leaders are visionaries who inspire and empower their teams to reach new heights. In the age of AI, this visionary leadership is going to be more critical than ever. We must be able to see the potential of AI, to imagine a world genuinely transformed by its possibilities, and to guide our teams toward that future. It's hard for most of us to truly understand the transformational potential of this new technology. By articulating a clear vision for AI adoption and demonstrating unwavering commitment to this vision, leaders can inspire their teams to take bold steps and overcome the obstacles that lie in the path of progress.

The foresight and pioneering mentality necessary for leaders in the AI era are personified in the Wizard's vision. By imagining a future where AI and humans work together harmoniously, the Wizard demonstrates the essential skill of embracing transformative technologies to solve complex problems. As a visionary leader, the Wizard's ability to plan for a thriving, AI-enabled world and inspire others to join the journey represents the strategic mindset needed for driving successful AI adoption and fostering a culture of continuous innovation.

AI CHAMPIONS & SUCCESS STORIES

- Recognize and empower team members who are enthusiastic about AI to become "AI champions."

THE WIZARD'S VISION   107

They can help promote the benefits of AI, provide peer support, and serve as role models to encourage other team members to embrace AI adoption, helping to shape and refine the vision everyone's striving toward.

- Share examples of successful AI implementations within your industry or other relevant sectors to help your team understand the potential benefits and inspire them to explore new possibilities.

- Ask team members to volunteer to bring their own examples to kick off staff meetings.

ORGANIZATIONAL VISION, MISSION & VALUES

- Clearly demonstrate how AI can support and enhance your organization's core mission and values, ensuring that AI adoption aligns with your overall strategic direction.

- Engage your teams to develop a clear and inspiring vision statement that outlines how AI will benefit your organization and its stakeholders.

INNOVATION CULTURE

- Encourage your team to imagine the possibilities and potential of AI within your organization. Foster a mindset of innovation and creative problem-solving.

- Encourage your team to be open to experimentation and learning from failure, creating an environment where new ideas and approaches are welcomed and embraced. (This is part of the culture of continuous education, focused by a vision of what could be.)

- Hold brainstorming sessions with your team to generate innovative AI-driven solutions that align with your organization's goals and objectives.

EXTERNAL STAKEHOLDERS

- Collaborate with customers, suppliers, partners, and other external stakeholders to gather insights and input on AI adoption, ensuring that your organization's AI strategy addresses their needs and concerns.

Chapter 7

THE WICKED WITCH OF RESISTANCE

"Are you a good witch or a bad witch?" – Glinda the Good Witch

I EAGERLY WATCHED THE texting bubbles on my iMessage window that indicated an incoming reply. I had shared a treat with a colleague – a clever, cool, and free online tool that would build a complete slide deck with just a few words to introduce the concept. I had tested it and loved it – it was truly "AI magic."

But then came his mocking response:

> lol, thanks but I'll pass. I can make my own decks.

What?! This man works for a tech consultancy, and his email domain is ".ai" – he **has** to embrace new technology! Doesn't he? Actually, no, he doesn't. (Though I expect he'll circle back in a few weeks to ask for the name of that slide-building tool.)

Resistance comes in all forms, but this mindset is where it begins. When smart, experienced people forget how to be curious, it often shows up as resistance.

Leaders often draw from a wealth of experience. It's generally an asset, but sometimes this makes us vulnerable to thinking we know what can't be done or what didn't work. I have some advice for the highly-experienced brilliant person reading this page:

The future is changing rapidly and hardly anything will be the same as it is now. In the New Oz, when we've trained ourselves to be explorers of **how** things work differently, we'll be more successful and lead happier teams.

FWIW, that guy never did his own decks anyway.

Leaders who are hesitant to embrace AI technologies may prevent their organizations from reaping the full benefits of AI-driven innovation. A prime example of an overly-cautious mindset is Kodak, a company that failed to adapt to the digital revolution in the photography industry. Kodak's leadership resisted change and continued to focus on traditional film-based products, even as competitors embraced digital technologies. As a result, Kodak – a world leader in its field for decades, with over a century of brand dominance – declared bankruptcy in 2012 after missing the opportunity to capitalize on the digital revolution.[49]

Adobe, in contrast, has proven to be a bit more flexible. They have a comparable creative user base and could have played it safe when generative AI emerged. Instead, they pushed GenAI deeply into Photoshop.[50] Adobe could have seen AI as a threat or distraction, but its leaders had the courage to invest aggressively in AI to elevate what users can do.

Companies like Netflix and Amazon succeeded, in part, because of their leadership's willingness to embrace change. Both organizations have unsurprisingly adopted AI technologies to improve their services and maintain a competitive edge. Netflix uses AI algorithms to personalize content recommendations,[51] while Amazon leverages AI to optimize its supply chain and logistics operations.[52]

The Wicked Witch of the West was feared for casting spells on all who dared to defy her. Her resistance to change and determination to hold onto power and control illustrate the barriers that can emerge with new ideas and innovations. In the context of AI adoption, the Wicked Witch symbolizes the forces that resist progress, fearing the potential loss of familiarity and authority.

As leaders guiding the AI journey to the New Oz, we'll confront our own Wicked Witch of Resistance – externally, inside our organizations, and even in our own thinking. The iconic Wicked Witch is a reminder that overcoming resistance is an important step in moving forward to embrace the transformative power of AI and other advancements.

Concern ≠ Resistance

"When you're a hammer, everything looks like a nail" is such a great adage. Be careful, because not all hesitancy or pushback is opposition. It's easy for those of us who lead these disruptive changes to get fatigued of managing the string of naysayers that line our path. Knowing the difference between oppositional defiance and those who are just expressing concern allows us to guide our teams with grace and empathy that supports stronger engagement and trust through the AI journey.

One of the things that keeps me grounded is to focus my attention on understanding where the pushback is coming from. I genuinely believe most people want to help and listening to their feedback often reveals their motivations. If their insights are delivered from a place of genuine care with a desire to see the organization succeed, they're just sharing concerns. The reasons people need to be heard are many and varied, but this is the easiest of fixes.

True resistance is rare and often comes from fear (fear of loss, fear of change, fear of missing out), plus a lack of knowledge. Getting to the root of why the resistance exists and enabling the person to solve the gaps themselves is often a solid turning point.

	CONCERN	RESISTANCE
Appearance	constructive provides valuable insights affords opportunities for improvement	unwilling to embrace change deep-rooted skepticism refusal to participate in the process
Stems from	a place of genuine care desire to see the organization and its people succeed	fear lack of understanding reluctance to let go of the status quo

It's a safe prediction that at least one team member will express concern about the impact of AI on their role or the roles of their colleagues. This concern is an opportunity for leaders to examine the specific talents of their team members and explore how AI can enhance those skills, instead of replacing them. It may present an opportunity to invest in upskilling or reskilling programs that help employees thrive in an AI-driven environment.

Data privacy and security are also shared concerns likely to surface as AI-enabled technologies become more common in the workplace. In this case, understanding the resistance may be more important than fixing it. It's hard to imagine an organization of any size not giving some level of consideration to security and data privacy through competent resources. My experience has been that most data privacy concerns are related to unconnected fears made worse by a lack of information. When employees are concerned about data privacy, there's an opportunity to get curious together and find out what information is available (policies, tools, training, etc.) as a solution to the issue.

Organizations can't really fix fear that's based on previous, unrelated events (for example, a large data breach at a credit card company), but we can help employees understand what we do to prevent similar events. Once we've worked to help make the information understood more clearly (including helping make the information more accessible to team members), it may be useful to ask the person to share an update with the team. **When resistance is converted to contribution, the investment gains grow faster and reach**

further. (Often, you have to create that opportunity — just ask.)

Successful Leaders Have Open Hearts and Big Ears

When team members express concern, it's important to respond with empathy, openness, and a willingness to listen. Creating a safe space for dialogue gives us an opportunity to address the concerns and gather important feedback to refine our AI adoption strategies.

As we journey through the web of AI adoption, it's critical that we listen closely to the subtle differences distinguishing our teams' valid concerns from simple resistance. The approach we choose to address these concerns sends a powerful message about our leadership and the direction we're steering our organizations. It's heartening to see that industry titans have taken a proactive stance on standards and regulations, garnering significant support in the process. Case in point: OpenAI's initiative to launch a grant program, inspiring individuals to think creatively and propose solutions to regulatory needs.[53]

Of course, not every organization can dispense $100,000 grants, but that shouldn't deter us. We're all capable of fostering an environment that invites input, messaging our eagerness to collaborate and proactively address any unease. Sometimes the best way to manage resistance is to shine a light on it and bring it out of the shadowy corners where it often hides. Tackling concerns head-on paves the way for enduring change. The point isn't just to react to resistance; we're actively inviting it into the dialogue to strengthen our course of action. With this approach, we'll transform resistance from an adversary to an ally.

Retaining Resistance: The Long Play

There are times when our attempts to be understanding and inquisitive only serve to nurture a lingering, vague sense of resistance. This sometimes happens with those who fear change but can't articulate why. A compassionate leader willing to lend an ear might provide an unintentionally vague solace, affirming their inaction. There's no one-size-fits-all approach to address this. My method? A blend of straight talk and tough love, which is admittedly not everyone's cup of tea. As I'm fond of quoting from Brené Brown, "Clear is Kind," and I find it inhumane to dwell excessively on uncontrollable factors or grand notions of potential risks that have been looming over us since long before AI came rolling into our lives.

In this world, there are individuals who hold the tangible parts of the system – a device, a software application – to an unachievable standard of perfection. Perfect products? I've yet to encounter one. Every product is subjected to imperfect users, engaged in flawed processes, fueled by data I'd rather not delve into. But what I've learned is: a product establishes boundaries that make our tasks substantially more efficient, scalable, and simply more useful than relying solely on human capacity. Given a choice? I'd choose the "product" every time, without a moment's hesitation. Some harbor a belief that AI is a failure if it isn't flawless. I've said it before, and I'll say it again – a world of absolute perfection is one I don't believe can exist. In this case, I'll take second-best.

Tackling the resistance of those seeking the unattainable can't be achieved by passive waiting: you'll find yourself stuck in an indefinite loop. Nor can it be resolved through endless listening. In such scenarios, it's essential to ask and expect more detailed explanations that lead to resolving their anxieties where possible.

In any fruitful conflict, it's essential all participants are committed to find a resolution – otherwise, it's just squandered time. With that commitment, the concern holding up should be specific – "global peace" is too vague a goal to strategize for. So is "Ethics," "Singularity," and "Regulations." If there isn't a more concrete problem you can lend a hand to solve, you're just pouring time into an unattainable solution because the resistor doesn't actually know what is needed to appease them.

Your personal technique for dealing with this will be based on your rapport with the individual and your own communication style. Help the person identify the core of fear, uncertainty, and doubt. Then, help them see the broader scope, for their sake and yours. There are other issues and teams that need your presence, so you simply can't afford to allocate unlimited time and effort to items that can't be narrowed down to a tangible addressable concern.

Loud Isn't Wrong

If things escalate and concerns are delivered by less desirable methods, don't lose sight of the fact that they're still someone's concerns. A colleague of mine leads healthcare technology for a large healthcare company. The last 10-15 years have been both transformative and difficult from a regulatory and technical perspective for clinicians in the field. The implementation of Electronic Health Records (EHR) systems has created a significant workload and divided medical teams by creating rules that segregate tasks and often counteract teamwork.

Recently, a more tenured staff physician had endured more than he could bear. He sent a scathing email to the entire hospital administration team outlining in painful detail the level of undesirable impact that the technology had created, and how it had placed a wedge between him and his patients. The email was thoughtful, but clearly written by someone who no longer wanted to participate in a different process than the one he had trained in for many years before EHR systems became necessary.

What impressed my colleague was the level of care the senior executives of this corporate medical system expressed for the staff physician. They treated him kindly and thanked him for taking time to provide feedback. They didn't minimize the email that had been sent or dismiss the claims of the challenges doctors face in delivering care and managing data input.

The hospital used the opportunity to educate clinical teams about the technology roadmap for the next 12 months (the roadmap had actually been published but was not frequently discussed). The administration also highlighted upcoming technology improvements in subsequent employee newsletters and video updates.

This might have been embarrassing or damaging behavior if the employee had been in other organizations, but this leadership team used the concerns as an opportunity to develop buy-in and trust. In the process, they did more than retain a single physician – their transparency re-engaged an entire workforce to be part of the go-forward solution.

And while we're talking about Healthcare...

> Since we just set the stage for this sidebar, this is a great spot to mention the possibilities we'll experience with AI in Healthcare. GenAI is a significant opportunity to address this physician's and countless others' concerns. AI will play an expansive role in transforming industries moving forward, and healthcare is a great example where this revolution will make a huge impact. In the last reported data, healthcare was the second largest category of corporate AI spend.[54] Imagine the power of utilizing AI to streamline processes, alleviate stress on our medical practitioners, and importantly – improve the patient experience. That would have been a real differentiator to change the story of our staff physician,

THE WICKED WITCH OF RESISTANCE

affording him the ability to focus on why he became a doctor: to heal and care for his patients.

In the New Oz, we're not just looking at the surface-level efficiencies AI brings. We're diving deeper into its potential to reshape our human experiences and interactions. Think of the time we could free up for physicians to engage with their patients – to listen more and offer comfort. These are the moments that can make a big difference in a patient's journey to recovery.

AI is also expected to have a significant impact on diagnostics. The medical world is enormous and always changing, with new studies, treatments, and discoveries emerging all the time. No single physician can be expected to retain every piece of information, every possible symptom or drug interaction – but with its immense data-crunching capabilities, AI can.

Imagine a world where each diagnosis isn't limited to the knowledge of one physician, but is instead augmented by a vast database of medical wisdom that is constantly updating, learning, and improving. AI will give healthcare professionals access to a breadth of knowledge far beyond their own experience. We'll provide insights gathered from countless sources, enabling them to make better, more informed decisions about patient care. This will be a level of accuracy and precision no individual could hope to achieve on their own.

And it's not only about patients. It's about giving our healthcare professionals the ability to practice their craft without cumbersome bureaucracy and logistical puzzles. AI can shoulder these burdens, giving our physicians back the time and mental space to do what they do best.

In essence, we're talking about using AI to reintroduce humanity into healthcare. By letting AI handle the paperwork and the data-crunching, we're freeing up humans to handle the human part – the empathy, the compassion, the moments of connection that can make the medical journey a little less daunting. That's the power of AI once we reach the New Oz.

It's not just about healthcare, of course. As we'll explore, the power of AI is universal – it allows us to refocus on the human aspects of every industry, to put people first. The efficiencies and improvements in our work are just the beginning. The true magic happens when we leverage AI to enrich how we connect, engage and ultimately, #leadwithlove.

The Antidote to Resistance: Involve, Inform, Educate, and Celebrate

Concerns expressed by our teams are not the same as resistance. Concerns are valuable opportunities for growth and improvement. By embracing concerns with empathy and openness, we'll create an environment where our teams feel seen, heard, and valued, so they'll be engaged throughout the journey of AI transformation. This collaborative and inclusive approach will lead us to create a brighter, more prosperous future in the New Oz.

The behaviors of empathy, wisdom, intelligence, and vision we discussed in previous chapters are foundational parts of an open and supportive culture. One of the best ways to overcome fear and doubt is to educate people about AI and involve teams in decisions that impact their work.

It empowers people when we help them understand what AI actually is and how it can be used to improve our lives. That knowledge and confidence places them in a far better position to identify use cases for improving their business and creates a cycle of engagement and trust that leads to success.

 People are more likely to trust the process and accept change if they believe that the people leading the change are trustworthy and credible. Develop a clear vision for how AI will be adopted and implemented, then be transparent about your intentions by communicating the plan and requesting feedback from others.

Training and building strong teams is essential for the success of any initiative, including AI adoption. When teams are well-trained and well-supported, they're more likely to overcome resistance to change successfully. Stronger teams are also capable of more effectively supporting each other on the journey.

Celebrating success is the most underperformed milestone in my leadership career history. When your teams achieve success, please make the time to celebrate their accomplishments. We're all moving too fast to the next milestone or project that is also moving too fast. Teams deserve our recognition and appreciation.

The Disagreeable Deserve Your Best Leadership

 I believe we would've made a difference for Miss Gulch (better known as the Wicked Witch of the West). No doubt, you'll have someone like her in your New Oz. Don't dismiss her... Educate her. Include her. Even let her hold your ruby slippers, because she cannot really steal your power. Resistance exists when people feel they're not being heard and they have no other options. We're all going on this AI journey together. The Yellow Brick Road may not always be an obvious path, but the future of work is for all of us. Including Miss Gulch. #LeaveNoOneBehind

AI Adoption ACCELERATORS

The Wicked Witch symbolizes resistance and skepticism that leaders encounter when introducing transformative technologies like AI. This resistance often stems from fear, uncertainty, or simply an unwillingness to adapt to change. Leaders responsible for AI adoption must recognize these challenges and proactively address them by supporting open communication, providing support and resources, and demonstrating the benefits of embracing AI. By actively working to anticipate, listen to, and counteract resistance, leaders will create a culture of adaptability and resilience, allowing teams to overcome the obstacles presented by the Witch and move confidently toward successful AI integration. Below are some of the practical things we can do to break the spell of Resistance.

Several activities already mentioned in previous Adoption Accelerator lists are also highly effective for lowering Resistance: **Conducting an AI readiness assessment** helps leaders understand employee skills and mindset. **Developing a clear communication plan** is necessary to give everyone an opportunity to understand the plans and direction. **Offering personalized training and resources** gets employees important exposure to new technology and builds confidence in their ability to transition work activities as technology evolves. **Appointing AI Champions** gives others in the business an opportunity to mentor

124   AI AND THE NEW OZ

and represent their business teams in important decisions about AI adoption programs. Other suggestions include:

CONNECT AI INITIATIVES TO CORE BUSINESS VALUES

- Clearly show the connection between the company's vision, strategy, plan, and related AI initiatives.

- Make sure that the company's core business values are fully aligned and supported by the AI initiatives the teams invest in.

INVOLVE TEAM MEMBERS IN THE DECISION-MAKING PROCESS

- Include team members in the decision-making process and they will feel more invested and less resistant to the changes.

ESTABLISH A FEEDBACK LOOP FOR CONCERNS

- Create channels for your team to share their feedback and ideas related to AI implementation. This will help you address issues that arise and demonstrates that you value their opinions and insights.

- Cover creative ideas received via this channel at staff meetings or all-hands meetings.

SHOWCASE EARLY WINS & SUCCESSES

- Share positive results and successes of AI implementation with your team (month-end email announcement? flyer hanging in a common area?).

THE WICKED WITCH OF RESISTANCE 125

- Build momentum and enthusiasm for AI adoption by highlighting how results have improved processes, increased efficiency, or contributed to better decision-making.

ADDRESS JOB SECURITY CONCERNS

- You know people are thinking about it, so address it as you can. Be forthright and direct with them. Update the details when you learn more.

- Be transparent about how AI adoption might impact roles and responsibilities and provide reassurance about your commitment to retain and upskill team members.

- Offer growth and development opportunities frequently.

RECOGNIZE & REWARD ADAPTABILITY

- Encourage a culture of adaptability by recognizing and rewarding team members who proactively embrace AI adoption, learn new skills, and share their knowledge with others.

- Make up a silly award name and pass the "trophy" around to the person who did something clever the next week — for example, Mr. Bendy with a "Gumby" doll as the trophy. Give the team a chance to speak up at each staff meeting to recognize someone who went above and beyond to be adaptable and let the team vote (informally, by cheering for the winner). The winner keeps Mr. Bendy at her desk for "bragging rights" until the next staff meeting.

DRIVE CONSISTENCY WITH GOVERNANCE AND OTHER USAGE STANDARDS

- If your teams use AI in a way that requires governance or some form of verified adherence, put those processes in place.
  If your team needs guardrails regarding when/how to cite AI usage, then ask a cross-section of your teams to develop and champion those recommendations.

- Avoiding conversations where people are inconsistent allows the inconsistency to grow to different areas of the business. It won't fix itself, because people will silo their behaviors, continuing to argue their points and staying inconsistent.

- Bite the bullet and make a decision. As Brené Brown says — "Clear is kind" — and teams benefit from clarity about expectations, even when they're tough to hear at first.

MONITOR PROGRESS & ADJUST STRATEGIES

- Continuously monitor the success of your AI adoption efforts.

- Address any emerging resistance and adjust your strategies as needed. This will help maintain momentum and ensure your team remains engaged and committed to AI adoption.

Chapter 8

THE MUNCHKIN LAND OF COLLABORATION

"My! People come and go so quickly here!" – Dorothy

IN A STRANGE BUT wonderful place, somewhere over the rainbow, our path takes us down a road paved with yellow bricks. As we look around, a new group of characters comes into sight, seemingly appearing out of thin air, their faces peeking out from behind multi-colored toadstools and exotic flowers. The journey through the strange and magical Land of Oz takes an intriguing turn as we meet the Munchkins for the first time.

The Munchkins: A Model of Collaboration

The Munchkins exemplify the power of collaboration. Their unity and willingness to cooperate with one another and Dorothy demonstrate how combining individual strengths and resources can lead to greater achievements. By working together, they not only helped Dorothy in her mission, but they also rid their land of the Wicked Witch of the East – creating a safer and happier environment for themselves.

The Munchkins, though diminutive in size, wield tremendous collective power. These denizens of the

Emerald City, in their charming and quirky way, bring an incredible wealth of collaboration and harmony to the place they inhabit. And in this collaboration lies a lesson, a beacon of hope, and a roadmap to a future of AI that is not divisive but instead brings us all closer, making our collective lives better, easier, and more connected.

The Land of Oz isn't the only place where this spirit of unity and collaboration can be seen. It was also exhibited in a pivotal chapter of our own history. Let's shift our focus from the Munchkins to a man who embodied collaboration and unity in this world, Dr. Martin Luther King Jr. The parallels drawn between the Munchkins and Dr. King may seem odd at first, but as their purposes come into focus, a significant similarity shines through – the power of collaboration.

Dr. Martin Luther King Jr – Leadership through Mass Collaboration

Like the Munchkins, Dr. King didn't tower over us with physical stature. He stood as a metaphorical giant, a colossus, with his ideals, his vision, and most importantly, his unyielding belief in the power of unity and collaboration. He brought together a divided and torn nation and painted a picture of a world where color didn't divide but enriched, where differences were not a cause for hatred but a reason to celebrate, and where love was not selective but universal. Dr. King's dream was not just his alone; he shared it, and it became a shared vision, a collective endeavor, and an inspiring example of mass collaboration.

Just as King rallied his followers in a peaceful, collaborative effort for equality, the Munchkins also understood the power of unity. They had endured the tyranny of the Wicked Witch and then welcomed Dorothy as their liberator after she inadvertently crash-landed her farmhouse and freed them from oppression.

But what does this have to do with AI adoption, you might wonder? I'll tell you...

Our current societal climate around AI is akin to a land ruled by the metaphorical "Wicked Witch" with fears, misconceptions, resistance to change, and a general mistrust about the implications of AI. Like Dorothy, we have an opportunity to change the paradigm and shepherd in a new era where AI is no longer seen as a threat but instead is viewed as a tool that enhances and improves our lives.

We can't do this alone. Dorothy couldn't have defeated the Wicked Witch of the West or made it to the Wizard without the help of her friends. Similarly, we need collaboration to unlock the full potential of AI. Collaboration between researchers and engineers, policymakers and business leaders, teachers and students – all sectors of society are necessary to ensure collective intelligence benefits everyone and the gap between the "haves" and the "have-nots" doesn't grow wider.

Picture this for a moment: a world where this collaboration on AI paves the way to breakthroughs that revolutionize healthcare. Think about a world where early detection of diseases becomes the norm, not the exception. Imagine a world where personalized learning through AI helps students across the globe have equal access to quality education. Envision a world where AI-driven sustainable solutions help us combat climate change effectively. It's a grand vision, isn't it? Just like Dr. King's dream.

One Voice, Many Echoes. In *The Wizard of Oz*, the Munchkins, each with their unique skills, perspectives, and voices, came together to guide Dorothy, protect her, and cheer her as she set out on her quest. It was not one individual, but the collective spirit of the Munchkins that made a difference, a beautiful example of collaboration getting Dorothy off to a solid start. (That song about the Yellow Brick Road is probably going through your head right now!...).

In our world, Dr. Martin Luther King Jr. mobilized a nation with his vision. A single man with a dream, he did not stand alone. He worked with people from all walks of life, leveraging collective strength to challenge and change the norms of society. He forged a path towards equality, drawing power from collaboration. Dr. King's "I Have a Dream" speech,[55] one of the most influential addresses in human history, was the pinnacle of his collaborative efforts. And the March on Washington where he delivered this speech wasn't about one man's dream – it was a collective dream, a collaborative dream, a dream that belonged to millions who yearned for equality and justice.

The Power of Shared Goals. Remember how the Munchkins were united by a shared goal in *The Wizard of Oz*? They wanted to live in a world free of the Wicked Witch and they all worked toward it, aiding Dorothy to help them achieve it. Similarly, Dr. Martin Luther King Jr. managed to unite people from diverse backgrounds with a common goal – the dream of a more equal, just society. He transcended cultural, racial, and economic barriers to instill a sense of unity, fostering collaboration on an unprecedented scale. His collaborative leadership showcased the power of shared goals, and this power remains relevant as we navigate the labyrinth of AI adoption.

NASA's Katherine Johnson: Collaborative Genius

Another powerful story about the impact of collaboration can be found with Katherine Johnson. Johnson's story, as depicted in the movie "Hidden Figures," is a testament to the importance of collaboration in overcoming adversity and achieving greatness. Johnson faced numerous challenges during her time at NASA, including racial and gender discrimination.[56] Nevertheless, she became a pivotal figure in the organization's success.

The story of Katherine Johnson, an African-American mathematician and "human computer" at NASA, mirrors the Munchkin's collaborative spirit. Johnson was part of the West Computing Group at Langley Research Center, a place where many African-American women found new job opportunities and a sense of belonging.

In a time when segregation and discrimination were prevalent, these women found strength in unity, collaboration, and mutual support. Their collaboration not only helped them break through barriers in their careers but also played a pivotal role in the success of NASA's space missions. As a group, these women regularly checked each other's work and ensured that no errors left the office.[57] They maintained a high standard of accuracy and reliability while they worked collectively to advance their careers and contribute to vital aviation research and space missions. This collaboration allowed the group to overcome barriers they faced and make significant contributions to NASA's achievements, including the successful launch of astronaut John Glenn into orbit.[58]

Lessons from Munchkin Land and the West Computing Group

Embrace Diversity: Just as the Munchkins and the women of West Computing Group each brought their unique talents and expertise to the table, leaders must recognize the distinct strengths AI can bring to their organizations, just like different employees. AI systems excel in areas like pattern recognition, data analysis, and automation of repetitive tasks. By collaborating with AI, leaders can access insights and capabilities that complement their own, enhancing decision-making and boosting overall productivity.

Foster Trust and Open Communication: Trust and open communication are essential for effective collaboration. The Munchkins' willingness to help Dorothy and the West Computing Group's commitment to accuracy and accountability are testaments to the power of trust. As AI becomes more integrated into the workplace, leaders must ensure that their teams trust the technology and are comfortable communicating openly with both their human and AI partners.

Encourage Mutual Support and Shared Learning: Collaboration thrives in an environment of shared learning, where individuals can support each other to grow and develop together. Leaders must foster a culture that encourages continuous learning, not just among human team members but also with AI systems.

By actively engaging with AI technologies and encouraging their teams to do the same, leaders can create a dynamic learning ecosystem where both humans and AI can continue to evolve together, adapting to new challenges and unlocking untapped potential.

Alliance Alchemy: Transforming Collaboration into Gold with the Flying Monkeys of Oz

Collaboration is an important skill for AI adoption, but the Flying Monkeys took collaboration and networking to a whole different level as they created alliances to combine their skills and resources to support their shared objectives. Though initially these objectives were dictated to them by the Wicked Witch, the monkeys were not intrinsically evil. They were equally capable of showing compassion and aiding Dorothy and her friends once the Witch's power was broken. They also demonstrated an ability to shift alliances based on mutual understanding and shared goals, a concept that leaders in our modern world should take to heart.

In the realm of AI, the concept of alliance-building is critical. Technology has made the world a smaller place, connecting us in ways we never thought possible. These connections create complexity and alliances are a key element of navigating this intricate network. Just like the flying monkeys, individuals, teams, and organizations need to form alliances to achieve their goals, whether it's developing new AI technology, implementing ethical guidelines, or navigating the regulatory landscape.

The flying monkeys also showed us that alliances aren't static; they can evolve based on situational context and mutual benefit. This is a valuable lesson for modern leaders. In an ever-evolving landscape shaped by AI, the alliances we build must be flexible and adaptable, ready to meet new challenges and seize emerging opportunities.

As the monkeys soared across the skies of Oz, they illustrated the power of alliances in reaching common objectives. They're a reminder that even when tasks seem impossible, forming alliances can broaden our capabilities and help us conquer adversity in ways we may not have expected. This lesson is particularly pertinent in our

AI-driven world, where challenges are complex, and no one will be able to go it alone.

Building alliances like the flying monkeys did involves understanding, respect, and the shared vision of a common goal. Leaders who can build these alliances, who can bring together diverse skills and perspectives and direct them toward a shared objective, are the ones who will lead us successfully into the New Oz.

Collaboration in the New Oz

Collaboration is a cornerstone of human progress. In the modern world, leaders face a new frontier of collaboration as AI technology becomes increasingly integrated into our daily lives. Like the Munchkins in Oz and the women of West Computing Group, leaders must embrace collaboration – not just with their human counterparts, but also with AI systems. As AI increasingly becomes fundamental to the modern workplace, understanding the power of collaboration and its impact on leadership will be increasingly essential.

The workplace is already wired for collaboration, and there's value in creating structure that supports collaboration leading to more effective execution with teams. My workplace responsibilities often include program operations across products, large-scale custom projects, and a myriad of activity that involves other organizations. Mike has led the Program Management Office function with me at two large companies during a period of significant corporate organizational transformation. Our secret sauce for leading these efforts was elevating communication and collaboration through the teams – but with more than a hundred active product releases in motion, we had to build an infrastructure to support it. Creating a consistent cadence that enables teams to stay aligned cross-functionally provides the connective tissue organizations need for support. Investing in operational tools and delivering consistent data broadly across teams is a conscious choice, and this transparency creates more opportunity for collaboration. Leadership should never be passive. Portions of our Yellow Brick Road may be impassable or unfinished, and it's our job to build the path so our teams focus on their deliveries (instead of the potholes) and stay excited about the New Oz they're working toward.

As we harness the full potential of AI-driven collaboration, leaders must recognize the importance of human collaboration and blend it with the capabilities of AI. This includes fostering an environment where team members are encouraged to share ideas, challenge assumptions, and work collectively to achieve common goals. AI has the potential to revolutionize collaboration by streamlining communication, automating mundane tasks, and providing insights that can enhance decision-making.

Collaboration: The Heart of AI

The value of collaborative intelligence increases as AI evolves. AI isn't about machines replacing humans; it's about humans and machines working together. It's about enhancing human capabilities, not eliminating them. Much like the Munchkins collaborated with Dorothy, Dr. King collaborated with the Civil Rights Movement activists, and the West Computing Group collaborated with each other and their NASA internal customers, we need to foster collaboration between AI and its human counterparts. By blending human creativity with machine efficiency, we'll unlock potentials we never imagined.

Creating a Collaborative AI Culture. The way the Munchkins accepted Dorothy and included her in their community and the way Dr. King inspired and included millions in his vision, highlights the importance of an inclusive, collaborative culture. They didn't hesitate to open their hearts and minds. To succeed in our AI journey, we'll need to cultivate this kind of culture. Establishing an AI culture that values collaboration requires leaders to create an environment where learning and adapting are encouraged. It demands a shift from the 'know-it-all' leadership to the 'learn-it-all' leadership, where continuous learning, like the unending Yellow Brick Road, is the norm.

Embracing Diversity – The Path to Innovation. Much like the colorful array of Munchkins, diversity fuels innovation. Each Munchkin, in their unique way, contributed to Dorothy's journey. Dr. King also harnessed the power of diversity, unifying varied voices under a common banner.

As we step into an AI-enhanced future, we need a diverse range of skills, perspectives, and voices. Tech-savvy engineers, visionary leaders, ethical watchdogs, educators, artists – everyone has an important role to play. Diversity of thoughts leads to better innovation, and in the realm of AI, innovation is not just beneficial but essential.

While navigating our AI journey, let's remember the Munchkins with their spirit of unity and their power of collaboration. Let's remember Martin Luther King Jr. and his dream, his fight, and his collaborative leadership. And let's remember the women of the West Computing Group who truly knew what it meant to help each other rise higher. Together, we can realize the full potential of AI, turning the challenges of adoption into stepping stones toward a bright, AI-enhanced future.

Collaboration is not just an option; it's the only way forward.

AI Adoption ACCELERATORS

The Munchkins and Flying Monkeys are fitting representations of how leaders can foster different kinds of collaboration and networking to promote AI adoption. Just as the Munchkins come together to create a supportive community and the Flying Monkeys form powerful alliances, leaders must establish strong connections both within and beyond their organizations. By fostering an environment of collaboration and building robust networks, leaders can harness the collective strengths and insights of diverse groups, ultimately accelerating AI adoption and driving innovation for the future. Below are a few ideas for how to accomplish those things.

SUPPORT COLLABORATION WITH TEAMS & TOOLS

- Hold frequent team meetings to discuss AI project updates, share successes and challenges, and collaborate on next steps and problem-solving strategies.

- Utilize digital platforms and tools to facilitate seamless communication, project management, and knowledge sharing among team members, regardless of their location.

REWARD COLLABORATION

- Acknowledge and celebrate the collaborative efforts of team members, reinforcing the importance of teamwork and cooperation in achieving AI adoption success.

INTERNAL AI INTEREST GROUPS & CROSS-FUNCTIONAL TEAMS

- Support the creation of informal groups or committees within your organization that focus on AI exploration, learning, and collaboration. Anything that supports AI culture being accessible in your organization is a step forward, even if it's relatively minor.

- Assemble a diverse group of team members from various departments to collaborate on AI integration strategies, ensuring that different perspectives and expertise are considered.

- Assemble a diverse team with members from different departments and backgrounds to ensure various perspectives and expertise are included in AI initiatives. Actively check in with those teams and support them to jointly develop proposals, align broad use cases, and develop grand ideas for how AI could do radical things to elevate the business.

HACKATHONS & INNOVATION CHALLENGES

- Host events that encourage teams to collaborate on AI-driven projects or solutions, fostering a sense of camaraderie and teamwork while also generating innovative ideas.

EXTERNAL PARTNERSHIPS & INDUSTRY EVENTS

- Accelerate your organization's AI adoption efforts by forming alliances with other organizations, academic institutions, or technology partners to leverage their expertise and resources in AI.

- Participate in AI-related conferences, workshops, and networking events to stay informed about the latest trends and best practices and connect with field experts.

Chapter 9

THERE'S NO PLACE LIKE HOME

"You've always had the power my dear, you just had to learn it for yourself." – Glinda the Good Witch

IT'S HARD TO IMAGINE that what we know today is only a fraction of what will someday be possible. Sam Altman shared his thoughts about the future[59] when he wrote,

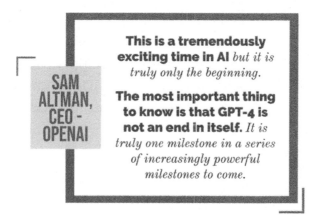

SAM ALTMAN, CEO - OPENAI

This is a tremendously exciting time in AI *but it is truly only the beginning.* **The most important thing to know is that GPT-4 is not an end in itself.** *It is truly one milestone in a series of increasingly powerful milestones to come.*

The most important takeaway from this book is that you have everything you need, *right now*, to lead your teams forward. Like Glinda the Good Witch told Dorothy, "You've always had the power, my dear. You just had to learn it for yourself."

Our journey is far from over; it's only just begun. As leaders, we carry the torch to light the way for others. We're pioneers in a land of immense possibilities and opportunities. Dorothy's return to Kansas in the original *Wizard of Oz* story is a powerful metaphor for the transformation leaders will undergo to successfully navigate our teams through the rapidly evolving world of AI, technology, and innovation. We're the ones who will help our teams navigate the Yellow Brick Road, overcome obstacles, and reach the New Oz of AI adoption. You have everything you need to get there. All you need to do is put one foot in front of the other (metaphorically speaking).

There will be more milestones. There will be technical milestones, economic and social milestones, and you will personally experience growth in your own ability to lead. But don't **wait** for any of those to happen. The key to moving forward is held by leaders who can galvanize teams to do new things. We'll learn different methods, change business practices, develop different ways of thinking – and we'll all grow.

Dorothy discovered during her journey through Oz that the power to create change and overcome challenges was always within her. The tools and skills **we** need to build a new ecosystem and create a better tomorrow are also already within each of us as leaders. Our role in the New Oz is not just to leverage AI and cutting-edge technologies for more efficiency, but to nurture our teams, our people, and our home – the organizations and communities we serve.

In our context, "home" represents the organizations we lead, the teams we manage, the customers we serve, and the societies we're part of. Our home is where we'll implement the learnings of this journey and where we'll witness the dawn of a new era, an era shaped by our partnership with AI.

Our "home" is not just about adopting AI; it's about evolving with it. It's about harnessing the collective intelligence of humans and machines to push the boundaries of possibility every day.

Dorothy's appreciation for home grew stronger after her adventure to Oz. As we forge pathways to new and unprecedented capabilities with AI, we need to always appreciate and remember the importance of human connection, empathy, and collaboration as we lead our teams to the New Oz. The magic that fueled Dorothy's journey came from her heart, her courage, her wisdom, and her ability to bring out the best in those around her. These same qualities are the foundation on which we'll build our AI-enabled future.

Make no mistake: our opportunity and responsibility as leaders in the New Oz is immense. It's our duty to cultivate an environment where innovation thrives and our teams feel empowered and engaged in the process of AI adoption.

We're going to have to do it together. We can't shy away from the challenges that lie ahead; we'll have to face them head-on using the knowledge and insights we've gathered during our journey. An influential Stanford professor offered these wise statements in a recent HBR article about pushing through fear to harness the power of AI innovation:

> Humanity never thrives when it fears innovation. Imagine if the first humans feared fire; yes, they got burned sometimes, but without harnessing the power of it, we might have gone extinct. We think the same applies to AI. Rather than fear it, we need to harness its power. We must put it in the hands of every human being, so we collectively can achieve and live at this higher level.[60]
>
> Benham Tabrizi and Babak Jahlavan
> *Harvard Business Review*

Dorothy's return home to Kansas signified a new beginning and a chance to apply the lessons learned from her adventures in Oz. Kansas may have seemed the same, but she was not. As leaders, we have the same opportunity to start fresh and apply the lessons learned from our experiences and history. Armed with the knowledge and insights we've gained throughout this journey, we'll be able to build a more innovative, collaborative, and prosperous future for everyone.

Embracing AI requires us to rethink and reshape our strategies, our operations, and our cultures at a level most of us haven't had to contemplate before. It requires us to be agile, adaptable, and open to experimentation. It requires us to embrace the unknown, take calculated risks, and always keep learning. The future is no longer on the horizon. It's here, and it's now. The cyclone has dropped us into a new land, and it's time to embrace that magical vision and set out to reach it.

Now is the time for us to take action and realize our role in building the New Oz. Let's embrace the transformative power of AI and other emerging technologies, while never losing sight of the importance of the relationships between our people, our teams, and our home.

I challenge you to take the next steps toward transforming your organization and building the foundation for the New Oz. Just as Dorothy embarked on her journey to return home, we'll embark on our journey to shape a future that honors the best of humanity and harnesses the potential of AI and technology.

As we move forward, we need to remember the importance of inclusion to identify and nurture talent. Dorothy assembled a team that was vital to her success, and she did it with an open mind and with grace. She got them to buy into her vision, and in doing so find what they were each searching for as well. In the New Oz, leaders will have the eye for talent that Dorothy had, recognizing potential in unlikely candidates and providing them with opportunities for growth and enrichment. We'll create a world where everyone contributes and their unique talents and perspectives are valued.

To reduce resistance and foster a culture of innovation and adaptability, we'll maintain open lines of communication with our teams, address their concerns, and involve them in the AI adoption process. We'll create a shared vision of the future that inspires and motivates our teams to embrace change and work together to turn that vision into a reality.

We won't build the New Oz in isolation. Collaboration and networking are crucial to our success. We'll forge alliances with other organizations, industry leaders, and experts in the field of AI to share knowledge, best practices, and resources. By learning from each other and working together, we'll create a strong, supportive ecosystem to accelerate the adoption of AI and drive the growth of our New Oz.

And finally, as we embrace our roles as leaders in the New Oz, we must recognize the power of our own hearts and empathy in guiding our decisions and actions. Our ability to connect with others, understand their needs, and champion their success will be the driving force behind the creation of a more sustainable, equitable, and inclusive future.

As you embark on this journey, always remember the power that lies within you. Like Dorothy, you have the heart, the courage, the wisdom, and the vision to overcome the challenges that lie ahead and build a brighter tomorrow.

THERE'S NO PLACE LIKE HOME 149

The ruby slippers are already on your feet. Use them to walk to your self-defined destination.

It's time for us to rise to the occasion and fulfill our responsibility to our teams, our organizations, and society. Together, we're the foundation for the New Oz to create a future filled with innovation, collaboration, and growth.

This shift is no small task. It's akin to moving mountains – but together, we have the strength to move these mountains. We are a community of forward-thinking leaders, a network of trailblazers who are ready to redefine the norms, to challenge the status quo, and to create a future where AI is not just a tool but a strategic partner.

As leaders, we'll harness our courage and bravery to make bold decisions and drive our organizations forward. We'll tap into our wisdom and knowledge to develop strategic plans for AI adoption that align with our organizations' goals and values. Our vision will help us anticipate the needs of our teams, our customers, and our industries, allowing us to stay ahead of the curve and proactively shape our AI-enabled future.

To achieve this, we need to continually invest in our personal and professional development. Embrace the spirit of the Scarecrow, whose quest for wisdom led him to uncover the innate knowledge and intelligence he already possessed. Keep learning, adapting, and growing so you can better serve your team and contribute to the development of the New Oz.

Like the Cowardly Lion, face your fears and take calculated risks to propel your organization forward. Lead with Love, like the Tin Man, keeping the human element front and center in your process and your vision.

In the New Oz, our vision must be clear and encompassing. We'll imagine a world where AI and humans work together in harmony, solving complex problems and creating a more sustainable, equitable, and inclusive society. Share this vision with your team and involve them in the planning and execution of your strategy. By working together, we'll create a future that benefits everyone.

As we close the pages of this book, remember the journey that Dorothy took to return to her beloved Kansas. She discovered the power within herself to overcome obstacles, forge friendships, and ultimately find her way home. We also have the power to create the New Oz, a place where our teams, our people, and our home thrive in harmony with technology and innovation.

Let's take up the challenge and step onto that brand-new Yellow Brick Road. Embrace your role as a leader in the New Oz, and use your heart, courage, wisdom, and vision to create a future filled with opportunity, collaboration, and growth.

The journey begins now.

Let's make it one to remember.

Ron Bates | Midjourney

Acknowledgments

"Oh, you're the best friends anybody ever had. And it's funny, but I feel as if I'd known you all the time, but I couldn't have, could I?" - Dorothy

Writing a book about the fastest-moving topic of 2023 was never envisioned as a solo project. Professional peers, Chief sisters, clients, Airstream familia, and others joined this expedition as we scoped the route of the Yellow Brick Road. AI *and the New* Oz was conceived, crafted, and launched in about 90 days. Despite the dynamic market and desire to publish, it was equally important to incorporate a few voices and their perspectives about how we collectively see a way forward in these uncertain times.

The team below generously supported this process. All left an indelible mark on the first edition of my first book. I'm grateful for how their input shaped the final product and enhanced the insights to make Oz more meaningful.

My deepest appreciation goes to:

GPT-4 and ChatGPT (3.5)

Ron Bates	Audrey Elliot	Carole Robin
Adam Carewe, MD	Russell Elliot	Laurea Salvatore
Cheryle Custer	Tracy Hill	Bruce Taub
Carla Davis	Catherine Houdek	Troy Trenchard
Danny DeCillis	John McGowan	Mike Lange Vera
	Elisa Camahort Page	

Thank you all, each and every one of you.

NOTES

Introduction

1. Amodei, Dario, and Danny Hernandez. "AI and Compute." OpenAI. May 16, 2018. https://openai.com/research/ai-and-compute.

2. Goswami, Rohan. "OpenAI CEO Sam Altman says he's a 'little bit scared' of A.I." CNBC. March 20, 2023. https://www.cnbc.com/2023/03/20/openai-ceo-sam-altman-says-hes-a-little-bit-scared-of-ai.html.

3. "Statement on AI Risk." Center for AI Safety. May 30, 2023. https://www.safe.ai/statement-on-ai-risk.

Chapter 1: The Yellow Brick Road to AI Adoption

4. Andreessen, Marc. "Why AI Will Save the World." Andreessen Horowitz. June 6, 2023. https://a16z.com/2023/06/06/ai-will-save-the-world/.

5. Prowe, Roen. "The Hitchhiker's Guide to Post-Post Modern Sapeocentrism." Snow Creek Advisory. May 3, 2023.

https://www.snowcreek.info/new-blog-1/2023/5/3/the-hitc hhikers-guide-to-post-post-modern-sapeocentrism.

6. Gates, Bill. "The Age of AI Has Begun." GatesNotes - The Blog of Bill Gates. March 21, 2023. https://www.gatesnotes.com/The-Age-of-AI-Has-Begun.

7. Clifford, Catherine. "Google CEO: A.I. Is More Important than Fire or Electricity." CNBC Make It. February 1, 2018. https://www.cnbc.com/2018/02/01/google-ceo-sundar-pich ai-ai-is-more-important-than-fire-electricity.html.

8. "AOL.com Company History Timeline." Zippia - The Career Expert. Oath Careers, Accessed April 3, 2023. https://www.zippia.com/oath-careers-33459/history/.

9. Gilbert, Ben and Sarah Jackson. "Steve Jobs unveiled the first iPhone 16 years ago — look how primitive it seems today." Business Insider. January 9, 2023 (updated). https://www.businessinsider.com/first-phone-anniversary-2 016-12.

10. "OpenAI.com Ranking." Similarweb. Accessed June 10, 2023. https://www.similarweb.com/website/openai.com/ #ranking.

11. Radauskas, Gintaras. "OpenAI CEO Won't Take It Public for Now: Investors Might Not Like "Strange" Decisions." Cybernews. June 7, 2023. https://www.similarweb.com/website/openai.com/#ranking.

12. "KPMG U.S. Survey: Executives Expect Generative AI to Have Enormous Impact on Business, but Unprepared for

Immediate Adoption." KPMG. April 24, 2023. https://info.kpmg.us/news-perspectives/technology-innovat ion/kpmg-generative-ai-2023.html.

13. Loten, Angus. "Inflection AI Raises $1.3 Billion in a Booming Market for Generative AI." WSJ.com. June 29, 2023. https://www.wsj.com/articles/inflection-ai-raises-1-3-billio n-in-a-booming-market-for-generative-ai-5954424c.

14. Wiggers, Kyle. "VCs Continue to Pour Dollars into Generative AI." TechCrunch. March 8, 2023. https://techcrunch.com/2023/03/28/generative-ai-venture-capital/.

15. Shaq, Wenqi and Eric Newcomer. "14 Charts That Tell the Story of AI Right Now." Newcomer.co. June 5, 2023. https://www.newcomer.co/i/123756524/at-least-generative-ai-companies-have-raised-more-than-million.

16. Hunter, Anne. "Executive AI Report." Hunter Marketing. March 30, 2023. https://huntermarketing.ai/marketing-insights/f/executive-ai-report.

17. Brecht, Rachel. As noted on LinkedIn. Countless occasions.

18. Peebles, Jamie. "What Services Will You Offer with the Help of AI?" LinkedIn (May 2023). Accessed May 17, 2023. https://www.linkedin.com/pulse/what-services-you-offer-he lp-ai-jamie-peebles.

19. Schwab, Stephanie. LinkedIn post, untitled. July 7, 2023. Accessed July 10, 2023. https://www.linkedin.com/posts/stephanieschwab_content-marketing-agency-2022-under-resourced-activity-7083060473344012288-fCZ9.

20. "The State of AI in 2022—And a Half Decade in Review." Quantum Black AI by McKinsey. December 6, 2022. https://www.mckinsey.com/capabilities/quantumblack/our-insights/the-state-of-ai-in-2022-and-a-half-decade-in-review.

21. "Great Expectations Study Reveals 77% of Organizations Have Data Quality Issues." Superconductive. June 16, 2022. https://www.prnewswire.com/news-releases/great-expectations-study-reveals-77-of-organizations-have-data-quality-issues-301569359.html.

22. "State of Data Report Emphasizes Emerging Shift to a Decentralized Model." Starburst Data. March 22, 2022. https://www.newswire.ca/news-releases/state-of-data-report-emphasizes-emerging-shift-to-a-decentralized-model-808230496.html.

Chapter 2: Dorothy's Eye for Talent

23. Robbins, Jane. "Richard Branson and the Virgin Group." Leadership Theory and Behavior, class blog for Vanderbilt University LPO 3450. November 3, 2009. https://leadershiptheory3450.blogspot.com/2009/11/richard-branson-ceo-and-founder-of-mega.html.

24. Knowledge at Wharton Staff. "The Importance of Being Richard Branson." Knowledge at Wharton. January 12, 2005. https://knowledge.wharton.upenn.edu/article/the-importance-of-being-richard-branson/.

25. Anderson, Erika. "11 Quotes from Sir Richard Branson on Business Leadership, and Passion." Forbes (online). March 16, 2013. https://www.forbes.com/sites/erikaandersen/2013/03/16/11-quotes-from-sir-richard-branson-on-business-leadership-and-passion/.

Chapter 3: The Cowardly Lion's Bravery

26. Brown, Brené. *Rising Strong.* New York: Spiegel & Grau, 2015.

27. Trenchard, Troy. Personal Interview with author. March 27, 2023.

28. Sukhija, Dushyant. *The Cisco Way: Leadership Lessons Learned from One of the World's Greatest Technology Services Companies.* North Charleston, SC: Create Space Independent Publishing Platform, 2016.

29. Graham, Paul. *Hackers and Painters: Big Ideas from the Computer Age.* Boston: O'Reilly Media, 2004.

30. Goeke, Niklas. "Hackers and Painters Summary." Four Minute Books. August 12, 2016. https://fourminutebooks.com/hackers-and-painters-summary/.

Chapter 4: The Tin Man's Heart to #LeadwithLove

31. Poulton, Geoff. "The former PepsiCo CEO is calling on business and government to help families thrive." October 24, 2022. Roland Berger; Think:Act Magazine.

https://www.rolandberger.com/en/Insights/Publications/Ind
ra-Nooyi-on-having-a-career-and-a-family.html.

32. Ward, Marguerite. "Why Pepsico CEO Indra Nooyi writes letters to her employees' parents." CNBC Make It. February 1, 2017. https://www.cnbc.com/2017/02/01/why-pepsico-ceo-indra-nooyi-writes-letters-to-her-employees-parents.html.

33. Vonnegut, Kurt. *Welcome to the Monkey House: A Collection of Short Works.* New York: Dial Press, 1950. "EPICAC" short story, published in November 1950 "Collier's Weekly."

34. Vonnegut, "EPICAC."

35. Korolevich, Sara. "Insights from American Workers: A Comprehensive Survey on AI in the Workplace." Checkr. May 24, 2023. https://checkr.com/resources/articles/ai-workplace-survey-2023.

Chapter 5: The Scarecrow's Quest for Wisdom

36. Khan, Sal. "How AI could save (not destroy) education." TED. May 1, 2023. https://www.ted.com/talks/sal_khan_how_ai_could_save_not_destroy_education/c.

37. Ignatius, Adi. "Alphabet CEO Sundar Pichai on Leadership, AI, and Big Tech." Harvard Business Review. HBR Ideacast. May 30, 2023. https://hbr.org/podcast/2023/05/alphabet-ceo-sundar-pichai-on-leadership-ai-and-big-tech.

NOTES

38. "Morgan Stanley Wealth Management Announces Key Milestone in Innovation Journey with OpenAI." Morgan Stanley. March 14, 2023. https://www.morgan stanley.com/press-releases/key-milestone-in-innovation-journey-with-openai.

39. Davenport, Tom. "How Morgan Stanley Is Training GPT To Help Financial Advisors." Forbes (online). March 20, 2023. https://www.forbes.com/sites/tomdavenport/2023/03/20/how-morgan-stanley-is-training-gpt-to-help-financial-advisors/?sh=4c7745003fc3.

40. "Morgan Stanley wealth management deploys GPT-4 to organize its vast knowledge base." OpenAI. March 14, 2023. https://openai.com/customer-stories/morgan-stanley.

41. Rotman, David. "ChatGPT is about to revolutionize the economy. We need to decide what that looks like." MIT Technology Review. March 25, 2023. https://www.technologyreview.com/2023/03/25/1070275/chat gpt-revolutionize-economy-decide-what-looks-like/.

42. Andreessen, "Why AI Will Save the World."

43. Vogels, Emily A. "A majority of Americans have heard of ChatGPT, but few have tried it themselves." Pew Research Center. May 24, 2023. https://www.pewresearch.org/short-reads-/2023/05/24/a-majority-of-americans-have-heard-of-chatgpt-but-few-have-tried-it-themselves/.

44. Beauchene, Vinciane, Nicolas de Bellefonds, et al. "AI at Work: What People Are Saying." Boston Consulting Group. June 7, 2023. https://www.bcg.com/publications/2023/what-people-are-saying-about-ai-at-work.

45. Korolevich, "Insights from American Workers."

46. Onion, Amanda, Missy Sullivan, et al. "This Day in History: February 11." The History Channel (website). Accessed May 3, 2023. https://www.history.com/this-day-in-history/nelson-mandela-released-from-prison.

Chapter 6: The Wizard's Vision

47. Yousafzai, Malala. "Malala Yousafzai." San Jose Speaker Series. San Jose Civic. February 14, 2023.

48. "Malala Yousafzai" speaker profile. San Jose Speaker Series. Accessed May 20, 2023. https://www.sanjoseseries.com/malalayousafzai.

Chapter 7: The Wicked Witch of Resistance

49. Bennett, Daniel. "Kodak Files for Bankruptcy." The Atlantic.. January 19, 2012. https://www.theatlantic.com/business/archive/2012/01/kod ak-files-bankruptcy/332934/.

50. Tabrizi, Behham and Babak Pahlavan. "Companies That Replace People with AI Will Get Left Behind." Harvard Business Review. June 23, 2023. https://hbr.org/2023/06/companies-that-replace-people-wit h-ai-will-get-left-behind.

NOTES

51. Matur, Vrinda. "Netflix's use of Artificial Intelligence Algorithms." AnalyticSteps. March 14, 2023. https://www.analyticssteps.com/blogs/netflixs-use-of-artific ial-intelligence-algorithms.

52. Rana, Anil. "How Amazon Uses Artificial Intelligence?" Seasia. January 3, 2023. https://www.seasiainfotech.com/blog/how-amazon-uses-art ificial-intelligence/.

53. Bensinger, Greg. "OpenAI offers $100,000 grants for ideas on AI governance." Reuters. May 25, 2023. https://www.reuters.com/technology/openai-offers-100000-grants-ideas-ai-governance-2023-05-25/.

54. NetBase Quid via AI Index Report (2022). "Annual global private investment in artificial intelligence, by focus area." Our World In Data. Accessed June 14, 2023. https://ourworldindata.org/grapher/private-investment-in-a rtificial-intelligence-by-focus-area.

Chapter 8: The Munchkin Land of Collaboration

55. Kakutani, Michiko. "The Lasting Power of Dr. King's Dream Speech." The New York Times. August 27, 2013. https://www.nytimes.com/2013/08/28/us/the-lasting-power -of-dr-kings-dream-speech.html.

56. Wu, Katherine J. "Smithsonian Curators Remember Katherine Johnson, NASA Mathematician Highlighted in 'Hidden Figures,' Who Died at 101." Smithsonian Magazine. February 24, 2020. https://www.smithsonianmag.com/smart-news/smithsonian-cu rators-remember-katherine-johnson-nasa-mathematician-dies-101-180974262/.

57. Dumbaugh, Della. "7 Things Students Can Learn from NASA Mathematician Katherine Johnson." The Conversation. February 26, 2020. https://theconversation.com/7-lessons-from-hidden-figures-na sa-mathematician-katherine-johnsons-life-and-career-132481.

58. Howell, Elizabeth. "NASA's real 'Hidden Figures.'" Space.com. November 11, 2022 (updated). https://www.space.com/35430-real-hidden-figures.html.

Chapter 9: There's No Place Like Home

59. Peter Lee, Carey Goldberg, and Isaac Kohane, Foreword by Open AI CEO, Sam Altman. *The AI Revolution in Medicine: GPT-4 and Beyond.* London, UK: Pearson, 2023.

60. Tabrizi and Pahlavan, "Companies That Replace People with AI."

About the Author

Tonya J. Long's career is a testament to the power of clarity, connection, and meaningful transformation in the workplace. With more than two decades of experience, she has served as a catalyst for change that drives significant economic impact by leading teams across more than 15 countries to restructure delivery models, integrate new talent and technology, cultivate executive teams, and shape fresh work cultures.

Secta AI Labs

In the dynamic and rapidly evolving field of generative AI, Tonya's history and expertise is indispensable. As a fractional executive, she helps companies navigate the complexities of AI adoption, bridging the gap between policies, governance, organizational use cases, and strategic initiatives. Her aim is clear: to help organizations successfully navigate the intricate landscape of company and customer-impacting changes, while moving confidently into the future of work.

Tonya's reach extends beyond her role as an advisor and thought leader regarding collective intelligence. She's the founder of an executive leadership placement and advisory firm and a board advisor to multiple organizations. As a member of CHIEF, the private network for women executives, Tonya's influence continues to grow into new geographies, newly evolving industry sectors, and via her mentorship of other executives. Her guiding principle is simple yet effective: deliver impact *When Needed, For the Time Needed, With the Skills Needed.*

Beyond her professional commitments, Tonya savors the thrill of the open road. You'll often find her towing "Bella Terre" – her beloved Airstream whose name translates to "beautiful lands" in several languages. When out with "Bella," she indulges her passions for hiking, photography, and of course, orchestrating family dinners with l*a familia de la corrientes de aire*, her Airstream family. You'll frequently catch her sneaking treats to other campers' dogs — a clear testament to her generous spirit.

Additional Resources

For information about upcoming speaking engagements, podcasts, and other resource material in development, please visit this community's website at https://www.ai-and-the-new-oz.com. You can also reach Tonya directly via email at Tonya@ai-and-the-new-oz.com.

A Request to Ask of You

Book reviews are pivotal for authors, especially those who are venturing into the literary world for the first time. As an author, reviews are the keys that unlock and validate your existence in a vast ocean of published work. Reviews also paint a picture of a reader who not only invested in purchasing the book but also devoted a moment of their valuable time to share their insights with the world. *Your words, thoughts, and perspectives matter more than you realize.*

You've journeyed through *AI and the New Oz*, and I'd be deeply grateful if you would leave a review on the platform where you bought the book. Even a few heartfelt sentences can make a world of difference. To simplify this, I've created some pointers you may find helpful at ai-and-the-new-oz.com/review.

Your honest reviews are the beacon that guides others to discover the book and join this empowering journey toward a new era of AI. If you are inclined to leave a review, please know that your effort truly matters. I appreciate your support and am so grateful for the people who have become part of this journey.

Made in the USA
Las Vegas, NV
29 February 2024